Deng Xiaoping

Book Design by Ian Robertson.

Edited by: Journalist Association, Chinese Non-ferrous Metal Industry
The Great Wall Publishing House

Originally Published in Chinese by: The Great Wall Publishing House

Library of Congress Catalog Number: 00-105179

Printed in China.
ISBN: 0-7643-1266-9

We are interested in hearing from authors with book ideas on related topics.

Published by Schiffer Publishing Ltd.
4880 Lower Valley Road
Atglen, PA 19310
Phone: (610) 593-1777
FAX: (610) 593-2002
E-mail: Schifferbk@aol.com.
Visit our web site at: www.schifferbooks.com
Please write for a free catalog.
This book may be purchased from the publisher.
Please include $3.95 postage.
Try your bookstore first.

In Europe, Schiffer books are distributed by:
Bushwood Books
6 Marksbury Avenue
Kew Gardens
Surrey TW9 4JF
England
Phone: 44 (0) 20 8392-8585
FAX: 44 (0) 20 8392-9876
E-mail: Bushwd@aol.com.
Free postage in the UK. Europe: air mail at cost.
Try your bookstore first.

Deng Xiaoping

Portrait of a Great Military Leader

Translated by You Rong & Xiao Wu

Schiffer Military History
Atglen, PA

Contents

Deng Xiaoping during the period of the Red Army.

Deng Xiaoping hurrying to the front of resistance against the Japanese aggressors.

Deng Xiaoping, the Deputy Director of the Political Department of the Eighth Route Army Headquarters.

Deng Xiaoping, the Political Commissar of the 129th Division of the Eighth Route Army.

Undertaking the important responsibility to lead the Anti-Japanese Base Areas in North China.

Deng Xiaoping, the Secretary of the Party General Front Committee at the frontline of the Huai-Hai Campaign and the Campaign across the Changjiang (Yangtze) River.

Deng Xiaoping, the First Secretary of Southwest China Bureau of the Central Committee of the Chinese Communist Party.

Deng Xiaoping, the Vice-Chairman of the Central Military Commission of the Chinese Communist Party and the Chief of General Staff of the People's Liberation Army.

Deng Xiaoping, Chairman of the Central Military Commission of the Chinese Communist Party.

Foreword

Comrade Deng Xiaoping is a prominent leader, outstanding proletarian revolutionary, statesman, and strategist with high prestige acknowledged by the Chinese people of all nationalities. As a military strategist, shouldered with pressing military duties, he is imbued with civil and military skills and has performed immortal feats for the nation and the people.

Comrade Deng Xiaoping is an important member in the leading collective of the first generation of our Party as comrade Mao Zedong was the core, and one of the principal leaders and founders of our army. In February 1927, after he returned to China from the Soviet Union, he was engaged in the political work among the troops of the national revolutionary army led by Feng Yuxiang, and thus began his practice of the revolutionary and military activities. During the period of the Second Revolutionary Civil War (1927-1937), he launched and led the Baise and Longzhou uprisings in Guangxi, founded the Seventh and Eighth Armies of the Chinese Workers' and Peasants' Red Army, and created Youjiang and Zuojiang revolutionary base areas. In the central revolutionary base area and during the course of the Long March, he implemented the correct line represented by comrade Mao Zedong. During the War of Resistance Against Japan (1937-1945), he at first became the Deputy Director of the Political Department of the Eighth Route Army Headquarters, then took the post of the Political Commissar of the 129th Division of the Eighth Route Army. Together with comrade Liu Bocheng, he led the troops to set up the Shanxi-Hebei-Henan base areas with the Taihang Mountains as their center, and co-operated with other anti-Japanese base areas behind the enemy lines to smash the attacks launched by the Japanese aggressors and recovered lost territories. In October 1943, he became the Acting Secretary of North China Bureau of the Central Committee of the Chinese Communist Party and was in charge of the work of the Eighth Route Army Headquarters. He was charged with important tasks to lead the Anti-Japanese base areas in North China in those hard times. During the period of the War of Liberation, he became the Political Commissar of the Shanxi-Hebei-Shandong-Henan Military Region to lead, together with comrade Liu Bocheng, the army and people in the Shanxi-Hebei-Shandong-Henan liberated areas to smash the invading and full-scale offensive to the liberated areas launched by Kuomintang troops. In 1947, he, comrade Liu Bocheng, and other comrades resolutely carried out the strategic decision made by the Party Central Committee on shifting the fighting from the interior front to the exterior front. With dauntless heroism, he commanded the troops to force their way across the Huanghe (Yellow) River, boldly advanced onward to the Dabie Mountains, and re-established the base area in the central plains with no rear support at all. In the following decisive battles with strategic importance, he, as the Secretary of the Party General Front Committee, together with leaders of the Central Plains Field Army (later called the Second Field Army) and East China Field Army (later called the Third Field Army), commanded the Campaign of the Huai-Hai and the campaign across the Changjiang (Yangtze) River, which wiped out the massive forces of Kuomintang army and liberated Nanjing, Shanghai, and a number of provinces in the southeast of China. After that, he led the troops marching forward to the Greater Southwest and liberated the cities of Guiyang, Chongqing, and Chendu, as well as four provinces of Sichuan, Guizhou, Yunnan, and Kangding, thus making possible the peaceful liberation of Tibet in 1951. Comrade Deng Xiaoping has gained ineffaceable merit for the independence of the nation, the liberation of the people, the founding and developing of the army, and the birth of New China.

In July 1952, comrade Deng Xiaoping was transferred from the Southwest Bureau of the Party Central Committee and the Southwest Military Region to the Party Central Committee and the central government. He became the General Secretary of the Party Central Committee, the Vice-Chairman of the National Defense Council, and a member of the Military Commission of the Party Central Committee. During his terms, he showed great concern for the building of the national defense and the army. He put forward a lot of correct suggestions on the work of army, participated in the making of many important strategic decisions concerning military affairs, and made an important contribution to the consolidation and strengthening of the national defense of New China. During the "Great Cultural Revolution," comrade Deng Xiaoping was deprived of all posts he held and was repudiated erroneously. After he was reinstated in his former office, particularly after he took part in the leading work of the Central Military Commission at the end of 1973 and became its vice-chairman and Chief of General Staff of the People's Liberation Army at the beginning of 1975, he waged a tit-for-tat struggle against the "Gang of Four" (consisting of Jiang Qing, Wang Hongwen, Zhang Chunqiao, and Yao Wenyuan). Under his leadership, a remarkable progress was achieved in the rectification of the army in a short period of time, and he won the wholehearted support from all ranks of the army. Later, he was once again wrongly dismissed from his leading posts of the Party, government, and army, but the movement of rectification of the army led by him played an important role, both in eliminating the adverse effects of Lin Biao upon the army, and in foiling the conspiracy of the "Gang of Four" to oppose the Chinese Communist Party, disband the army, and to usurp the leadership of the Party.

After the convening of the Third Plenary Session of the Eleventh Party Central Committee, comrade Deng Xiaoping became the core of the leading collective of the second generation of our Party and the commander of our army. Together with other leading members of the Central Military Commission, he called on the people to liberate the mind, seek truth from facts, bring order out of chaos, learn from the past, and open up the future. He summarized and put forward the concept for building the army in the new era; took a leading part in formulating a series of guiding principles and policies for building the army; and presented a set of scientific military theories with Chinese characteristics. Under the new historical condition, he maintained and developed Mao Zedong's military thought. Showing great foresight, he presented an important view that a new world war could be postponed and prevented. Accordingly, he made the important decisions on a strategic transformation of the guiding principles for the building of our army, i.e. reducing military strength by one million and allowing the national defense industry, which used to manufacture military products, to manufacture civilian products. He advocated the strategic principle of active defense, stressing the upholding and development of the theory of people's war under the conditions of modern times. In order to keep the correct direction in the army modernization process, he reiterated the importance of upholding the four basic principles (that is: the socialist path, proletarian dictatorship, leadership of the Communist Party, and Marxism-Leninism and Mao Zedong Thought) and the importance of maintaining the nature of the people's army. He demanded that the army should always be under the absolute leadership of the Party. He paid much attention to improving the army's combat effectiveness, listed the training and education work of the army as a strategic priority, and stressed the strengthening and improvement of the political work in the army. He emphasized that the army should be commanded according to the law and managed strictly. The leadership ranks and cadres' qualities of the army should be improved. He devoted much attention to the logistic support, the improvement of weaponry and equipment, the building of reserve forces, the research and development of highly sophisticated science and technology, and the research of military science. Under the new historical conditions, he pointed out that the relationships between the national defense and the building of the army and the economic construction should be correctly handled, stressing that the army should be in every aspect subjected to and serve the overall goal of national construction. He demanded that the army should actively support and take part in the national economic construction and make great efforts to the training of dual-purpose talents (persons to be trained by the Chinese People's Liberation Army with skills in both military fighting and economic construction) so as to coordinate the development between the national defense, the building of the army, and the economic construction. Under the correct guidance by the Party Central Committee and Central Military Commission with comrade Deng Xiaoping as their core, our army has steadily gotten onto the right track, focusing on its modernization, and therefore has achieved a remarkable progress. This has opened a new page in the military history of the socialist new China. The practice in the past dozen years has shown that comrade Deng Xiaoping is not only a chief architect for China's reform and opening up to the outside world in the course of socialist modernization, but also he fully deserves the same title for all aspects of the army's work, including the building of the national defense in the new period in China.

In November 1989, proceeding from the consideration of the fundamental interests of the Party, the nation, and the army, comrade Deng Xiaoping resigned, of his own will, from the post of Chairman of the Central Military Commission of Chinese Communist Party, fulfilling his wishes to withdraw completely from the leading posts. This shows the open-mindedness, profound vision, and sagacity of a great proletarian revolutionary and a military strategist. Although comrade Deng Xiaoping retired from the leading post of the army, his thought and theory on the building of national defense and the army in the new period are an integral component of the theory on building socialism in China with the Chinese characteristics, and still serve as the framework for the building of the army in peaceful time and as guidelines for various kinds of work in the army.

Pictorial on Deng Xiaoping's Military Activities

The Starting Point of the Military Activities

1. Ancient city, Xi'an.

At the end of 1926, on the instruction from the Party Central Committee, Deng Xiaoping and some 20 other comrades returned to China from Moscow. They were deployed as part of the troops led by General Feng Yuxiang, who asked the Communist Party to dispatch its staff to work in his troops. Not long after arriving at Ulan Bator in Mongolia, Deng Xiaoping, Wang Chongyun, and Zhu Shiheng composed as an advance team, first boarded a truck loaded with ammunitions which were supplied by the Soviet Union to Feng Yuxiang's forces. And then they switched to ride camels and horses. They pressed on day and night for more than two months and reached Xi'an in February, 1927. Before long, Deng Xiaoping was sent by the Party organization to Xi'an Zhongshan (Sun Yat-sen) Military School to be the Chief of the Political Section and the political science instructor, concurrently. He was also the Secretary of Party organization in the school.

In terms of structure, Zhongshan Military School was affiliated with the Shaanxi Headquarters of the National Allied Forces led by Feng Yuxiang, but in fact, it was directly led and controlled by the Communist Party. It was founded jointly by a Kuomintang left-winger, Yu Youren, and two Communists, Liu Bojian and Shi Kexuan. It enjoyed the high reputation of being "Whampoa Military Academy in the Northwest." The school offered various courses of political science, such as "An Introduction to Socialism," "ABCs of Communism," "The Nation and the Revolution," and "The New Three Principles of the People (i.e. Nationalism, Democracy, and the People's Livelihood put forward by Dr. Sun Yat-sen)." Deng Xiaoping personally gave lectures on the principles of Marxism and Leninism to cadets, and advocated revolutionary thought among them. He also made arrangements for some Communist Party members to come to the school in the capacity of the members of Kuomintang to carry out revolutionary activities.

At the end of June, 1927, due to Feng Yuxiang's policy of "asking the Communist Party members to leave the province in courtesy," Deng Xiaoping left Xi'an for Wuhan via Zhengzhou. He was assigned by the Party organization to be a secretary in the Party Central Committee.

On August 7, 1927, Deng Xiaoping, as a non-voting delegate, attended the emergency meeting of the Party Central Committee presided over by Qu Qiubai. This meeting corrected the mistakes of Right opportunism made by Chen Duxiu, established the general principles of carrying out the agrarian revolution and armed struggle against Kuomintang reactionaries, and also decided to dispatch the experienced cadres to some provinces and regions for the purpose of organizing the peasants' uprisings. Subsequently, the offices of the Party Central Committee were relocated secretly to Shanghai, and Deng went with them. In December 1927, Deng Xiaoping became the Secretary General of the Party Central Committee.

2

3

4

2. In order to find out the truth of how to save the nation, Deng Xiaoping went to France to work his way through college. During this period of study abroad, Deng Xiaoping embraced Marxism. The photo shows Deng Xiaoping in Lyon, France.

3. In January 1926, Deng Xiaoping left France for the Soviet Union and entered Zhongshan (Sun Yat-sen) University, Moscow. His study there laid a foundation in his ideology for his future military activities. This is the site of the former Zhongshan University.

4. In the spring of 1927, Deng Xiaoping returned to China from the Soviet Union. On instruction from the Party, he went to Xi'an Zhongshan Military School, which was affiliated with the National Allied Forces led by Feng Yuxiang. Deng took the posts of Chief of the Political Section and instructor of political science, and thus began his military career. The photo shows a mass pledge rally held at Wuyuan by the National Allied Forces to support the Northern Expedition (1926-1927).

5. On August 7, 1927, Deng Xiaoping, as a non-voting delegate, attended the emergency meeting (i.e. Meeting of August 7) of the Party Central Committee presided over by Qu Qiubai in Hankou. This is the conference room of the "Meeting of August 7."

6. The minutes of the "Meeting of August 7," which Deng Xiaoping attended as a non-voting delegate.

5

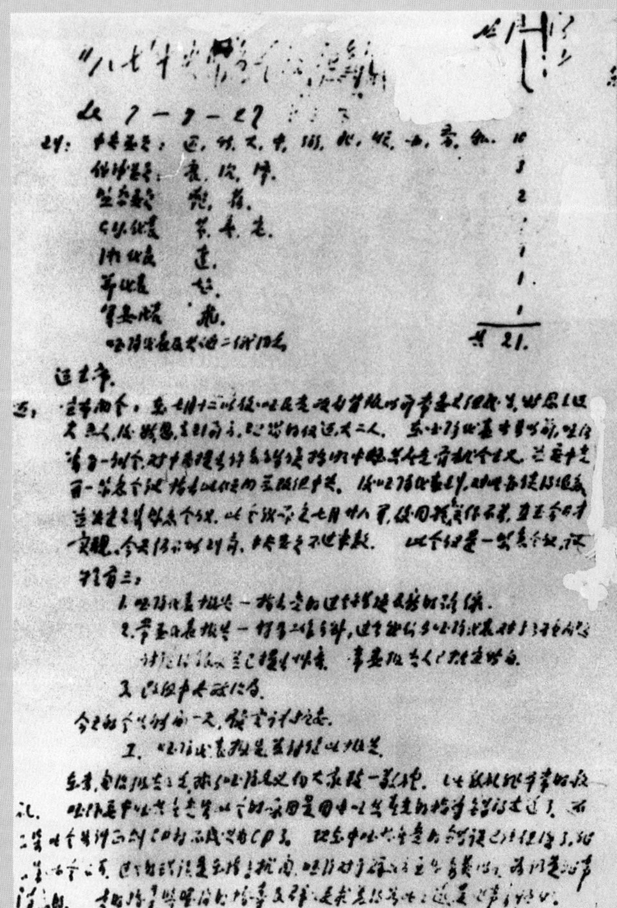

6

Launching and Leading the Armed Uprisings & Founding the Seventh and Eighth Armies of the Red Army

1. Deng Xiaoping, the Political Commissar of the Seventh and Eighth Armies of the Chinese Workers' and Peasants' Red Army.

In July 1929, as the representative of the Party Central Committee, Deng Xiaoping went to Guangxi to carry out activities for the united front, soldier's movement, and peasant's movement in preparations for the armed uprisings. This was the first time he took the leading responsibility independently for a strategic area. In October, together with Zhang Yunyi, Deng Xiaoping led the fourth and fifth garrison battalions and the training regiment to Baise, Tianzhou Town, and Nabo Town of Fengyi County in the Youjiang area. In Baise, Deng Xiaoping presided over a joint meeting of the Party Special Committee and Military Commission of Guanxi. At the meeting, a decision was made on making appropriate preparations for the armed uprisings, and for establishing the Red Army and the Soviet government.

In early November 1929, after receiving the Party Central Committee's decision on approving the plan of holding the armed uprisings in Zuojiang and Youjiang areas and the decision on establishing the Guangxi Party Front Committee with Deng Xiaoping as its secretary, Deng Xiaoping immediately held a meeting of the Party Front Committee at Yuedong Guild Hall in Baise. At that meeting, he gave a briefing on the essence of directives of the Party Central Committee to the participants and formulated a detailed plan on Baise armed uprising.

In late November 1929, the Party Central Committee summoned Deng Xiaoping by telegram to Shanghai to report his work in Guangxi. On his way, Deng Xiaoping stopped at Longzhou and chaired a meeting of local cadres from the Party, Soviet government, and the Red Army. He briefed them about the decisions made by the Party Central Committee on holding the Zuojiang uprising and establishing the Eighth Army of the Red Army, as well as the decision on trying to launch the Longzhou uprising in a short period of time.

In December 1929, together with Zhang Yunyi and others, Deng Xiaoping led and launched the Baise uprising, founded the Seventh Army of the Chinese Workers' and Peasants' Red Army, and established the Youjiang Soviet Government. Deng Xiaoping became the Political Commissar of the Seventh Army.

On February 1, 1930, in accordance with the arrangements made by Deng Xiaoping and the Party Front Committee, the Longzhou uprising was launched, and both the Eighth Army of the Chinese Workers' and Peasants' Red Army and Zuojiang Soviet government were established. Deng Xiaoping became the Political Commissar of the Eighth Army concurrently. On February 7, Deng Xiaoping came back to Longzhou from Shanghai, transmitted to the local cadres the relevant directives given by the Party Central Committee, and founded the Provisional Party Front Committee of the Eighth Army.

In March 1930, Deng Xiaoping chaired a meeting of the Party Front Committee of the Seventh Army at Panyangyu, Fengshan County, at which a decision was made that the main forces of the Seventh Army be deployed to the border region of Guizhou and Guangxi to establish a guerrilla area. After the main forces of the Seventh Army withdrew from the Youjiang base area, Deng Xiaoping and Wei Baqun lived at Kuixing (the four stars in the bowl of the Big Dipper) Tower, Donglan County. In this place they often held meetings, and discussed and elaborated on the detailed policies and measures for carrying out the agrarian revolution in the Zuojiang and Youjiang base areas.

In May 1930, Deng Xiaoping went to Hechi to meet the main forces of the Seventh Army returning from Guizhou. In early June, Deng Xiaoping himself led the troops to attack Baise, where the defense force was relatively weak. After a 4-hour fierce battle, the enemy was completely defeated. Afterwards, Deng Xiaoping directed his troops to march eastward, and successively recovered Fengyi and Enlong along the bank of the Youjiang River, connecting them with Donglan, Fengshan, and other areas.

At the end of September 1930, Deng Gang, a representative from the Southern Bureau of the Party Central Committee, came to Youjiang area to transmit the resolution adopted by the meeting of the Political Bureau of the Party Central Committee on June 11, 1930, as well as the directives given by the Southern Bureau on September 3, 1930, to the Party Front Committee of the Seventh Army. He demanded the Seventh Army adopt the "Leftist" Lisan (Li Lisan, 1899-1967, the then leader of the Chinese Communist Party) Line. Though Deng Xiaoping presented his differing viewpoint, he obeyed the orders from his superiors, since he took the interests of the whole into account.

In February 1931, under the command of Deng Xiaoping and Li Mingrui, a part of the Seventh Army went to Chongyi County, Jiangxi Province, to lead and carry out the work of reconstructing and re-establishing the Party organizations there. In early March, Deng Xiaoping went to Shanghai to report his work to the Party Central Committee. In July, the Seventh Army joined the forces of the Third Army Group led by Peng Dehuai at Qiaotou Town, Xingguo County.

2

3

4

2. Baise, Guangxi.

3. Deng Xiaoping held a meeting of the Party Front Committee at Yuedong Guild Hall in Baise and formulated a detailed plan on the Baise uprising. This is the site of the former Guild Hall.

4. Zhang Yunyi, the Commander of the Seventh Army of the Chinese Workers' and Peasants' Red Army.

5

6

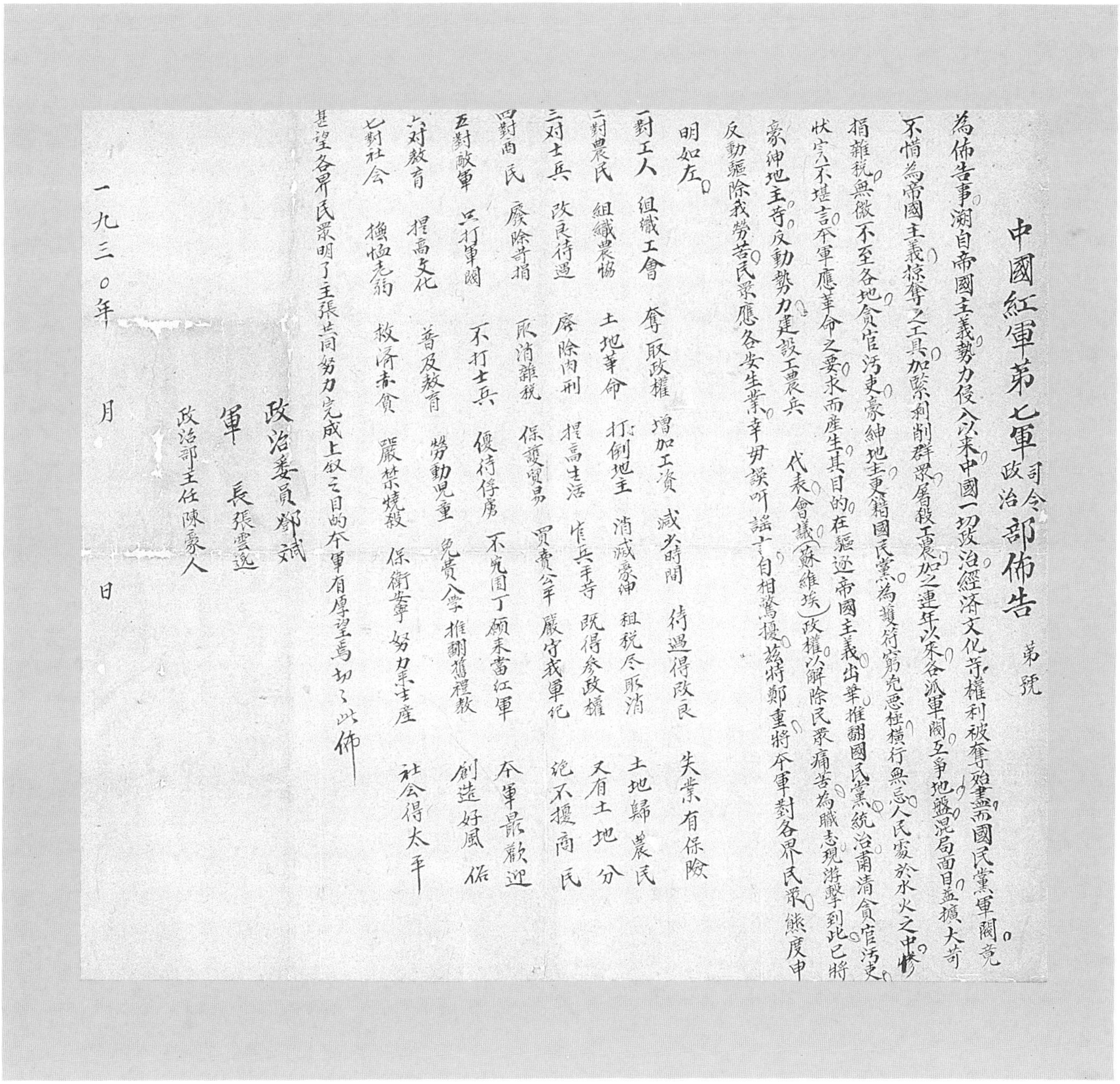

中國紅軍第七軍司令政治部佈告 第 號

為佈告事溯自帝國主義勢力侵入以来中國一切政治經济文化等權利被奪殆盡而國民黨軍閥竟不惜為帝國主義掠奪之工具加緊剝削群眾屠殺工農加之連年以來各派軍閥互爭地盤混局面目益擴大苛捐雜稅無微不至各地貪官污吏豪紳地主更藉國民黨為護符窮兇惡極橫行無忌人民處於水火之中慘狀實不堪言本軍應革命之要求而產生其目的在驅逐帝國主義出華推翻國民黨統治肅清貪官污吏豪紳地主等反動勢力建設工農兵代表會議(蘇維埃)政權以解除民眾痛苦為職志現游擊到此已將反動驅除我勞苦民眾應各安生業幸毋誤听謠言自相驚擾茲特鄭重將本軍對各界民眾態度申明如左

一對工人 組織工會 奪取政權 增加工資 減少時間 待遇得改良 失業有保險

二對農民 組織農協 土地革命 打倒地主 消滅豪紳 租稅盡取消 土地歸農民

三对士兵 改良待遇 廢除肉刑 提高生活 准兵平等 既得參政權 又有土地分

四對商民 廢除苛捐 取消雜稅 保護貿易 買賣公平 嚴守我軍紀 絕不擾商民

五對敵軍 只打軍閥 不打士兵 優待俘虜 不究團丁 倘來當紅軍 本軍最歡迎

六对教育 提高文化 普及教育 勞動兒童 免費入學 推翻舊禮教 創造好風俗

七對社会 撫恤老弱 救濟赤貧 嚴禁燒殺 保衛安寧 努力求生產 社会得太平

甚望各界民眾明了主張共同努力完成上叙之目的本軍有厚望焉切切此佈

政治委員鄧斌
軍 長張雲逸
政治部主任陳豪人

一九三〇年 月 日

7

5. The bedroom and office at Yuedong Guild Hall shared by Deng Xiaoping and Zhang Yunyi.

6. The site of the former Youjiang Soviet Government established after the Baise uprising.

7. The notice issued by the Command and the Political Department of the Seventh Army. In the notice, the Political Commissar Deng Bin is the alias of Deng Xiaoping.

8

8. Both Deng Xiaoping and Wei Baqun lived at Kuixing Tower in Wuzhuan District, Donglan County. They often held meetings of leading cadres here, as well as discussed and elaborated the detailed policies and measures on carrying out the agrarian revolution in the Zuojiang and Youjiang areas.

The Red Army in the Period Before and After the Long March

(a major strategic movement of the Chinese Workers' and Peasants' Red Army which succeeded in reaching the revolutionary base in northern Shaanxi after traversing eleven provinces and covering 25,000 li, or 12,500 kilometers, 1934-1935).

1. The Luding Bridge crossed by the Red Army during the Long March.

In the summer of 1931, Deng Xiaoping became the Secretary of the Party Committee of Ruijin County. He corrected the deviation made in the movement of "elimination of counterrevolutionaries" in the early period, held a Conference of the Soviet Delegates from the whole county, carried out the mass movement of saving food, supported the front, and made great efforts to develop agricultural production. Therefore, the situation of the county was greatly improved.

In July 1932, Deng Xiaoping was transferred to be the Secretary of the Party Committee of Huichang Central County, and concurrently the Political Commissar of the Third Military Sub-region of Jiangxi Provincial Military Region. In 1933, he was transferred again to be the Director of the Propaganda Department of the Jiangxi Provincial Party Committee. At that time, the Provisional Central Committee of the Chinese Communist Party carried out the "Leftist" dogmatism. After it was relocated to the Central Chinese Soviet Areas, a struggle against the "Luo Ming Line (Luo Ming, the then Secretary of the Party Committee of Fujian Province)" was unfolded. Deng Xiaoping, Mao Zetan, Xie Weijun, and Gu Bai were repudiated only because they implemented the correct line represented by Mao Zedong and opposed the "Leftist" erroneous leadership headed by Wang Ming. In May 1933, Deng Xiaoping was dismissed from the post of Director of the Propaganda Department and was transferred to be an inspector in a remote place called Nanchun Village in Le'an County. Before long, he was transferred once again to be the Secretary General of the General Political Department of the Red Army.

In August 1933, Deng Xiaoping was the editor-in-chief of Red Star, the official newspaper of the General Political Department of the Red Army.

In October 1934, Deng Xiaoping led the staff of Red *Star* to take the Long March with the column of the Central Military Commission. During the March, they encountered lots of fierce fighting and hardships. Deng led his staff to overcome all kinds of difficulties in order to continue the editing and publication of the *Red Star* newspaper. The newspaper transmitted in time to the officers and men the plan adopted by the Central Revolutionary Military Commission on military operations and deployment, disseminated the encouraging deeds of fellow officers and men of the Red Army, and advocated the Party's principles and policies, as well as the Red Army's aims and tasks. Thus, it became both an important mouthpiece of the Party Central Committee and the Central Revolutionary Military Commission and the spiritual food for the soldiers of the Red Army during the Long March.

In January 1935, in the capacity of the Secretary General of the Party Central Committee, Deng Xiaoping attended the Zunyi Meeting, which was a significant turning point in the history of our Party, and he supported the correct propositions raised by Mao Zedong. Later, when he evaluated the historical merits and contributions of the Zunyi Meeting, he said that the central leadership matured after Mao Zedong was affirmed as its core at the Zunyi Meeting held in 1935.

After the Zunyi Meeting, under the wise leadership of Mao Zedong and others, the Central Red Army implemented the flexible strategies and tactics, galloping with ease in Guizhou and Yunnan provinces. They crossed the Chishui River four times, and in early May 1935 crossed the Jinsha River. They finally jumped out of besiegement, pursuance, obstruction, and interception by hundreds of thousands of Kuomintang troops and won the victory with decisive significance in the strategic transfer. Later, Deng Xiaoping said that crossing the Chishui River four times was a brilliant page in Mao Zedong's military thought.

In June 1935, the Central Red Army victoriously joined the forces of the Fourth Front Army at Maogong district, western Sichuan Province. In July, Deng Xiaoping was assigned on instruction to be the Chief of the Propaganda Division in the Political Department of the First Army Group of the Red Army.

After the Mao'ergai Meeting, Deng Xiaoping and the officers and men of the First Army Group surmounted various difficulties and hardships by fighting against the wind, snow, and bitter cold, trudging the marshland and clambering the snowy mountains. They resolutely supported the Party Central Committee's principles of going north to fight against the Japanese aggressors and opposed the line of retreat to the south advocated by Zhang Guotao. During these extremely adverse circumstances, Deng paid special attention to the mass mobilization work, requiring the officers and soldiers of the Red Army to strictly maintain the disciplines.

In December 1935, the Party Central Committee held an enlarged meeting of its Political Bureau at Wayaobao, northern Shaanxi. Decisions were made at the meeting on establishing a broadest-based national united front to fight against Japanese aggressors, and on setting up the Anti-Japan Advance Army of the Chinese People's Red Army, which consisted of the First Army Group, the Fifteenth Army Group, and the Twenty-eighth Army led by Liu Zhidan.

On February 20, 1936, Deng Xiaoping and the Anti-Japan Advance Army went to cross the Yellow River from the west bank and entered into Shanxi Province, making preparations to fight directly against the Japanese troops. In Shanxi, the advance army was instead intercepted and attacked by heavy forces of Kuomintang troops. In order to be united as one in combating the Japanese, the anti-Japan advance army withdrew as ordered to the west bank of the Yellow River on May 5. Returning from the east expedition, Deng Xiaoping became the Deputy Director of the Political Department of the First Army Group of the Red Army, and soon afterwards, he was promoted to be its director.

2

2. The site of the former General Political Department of the Red Army.

3. Dend Xiaoping was the editor-in-chief of the newspaper, *Red Star.*

3

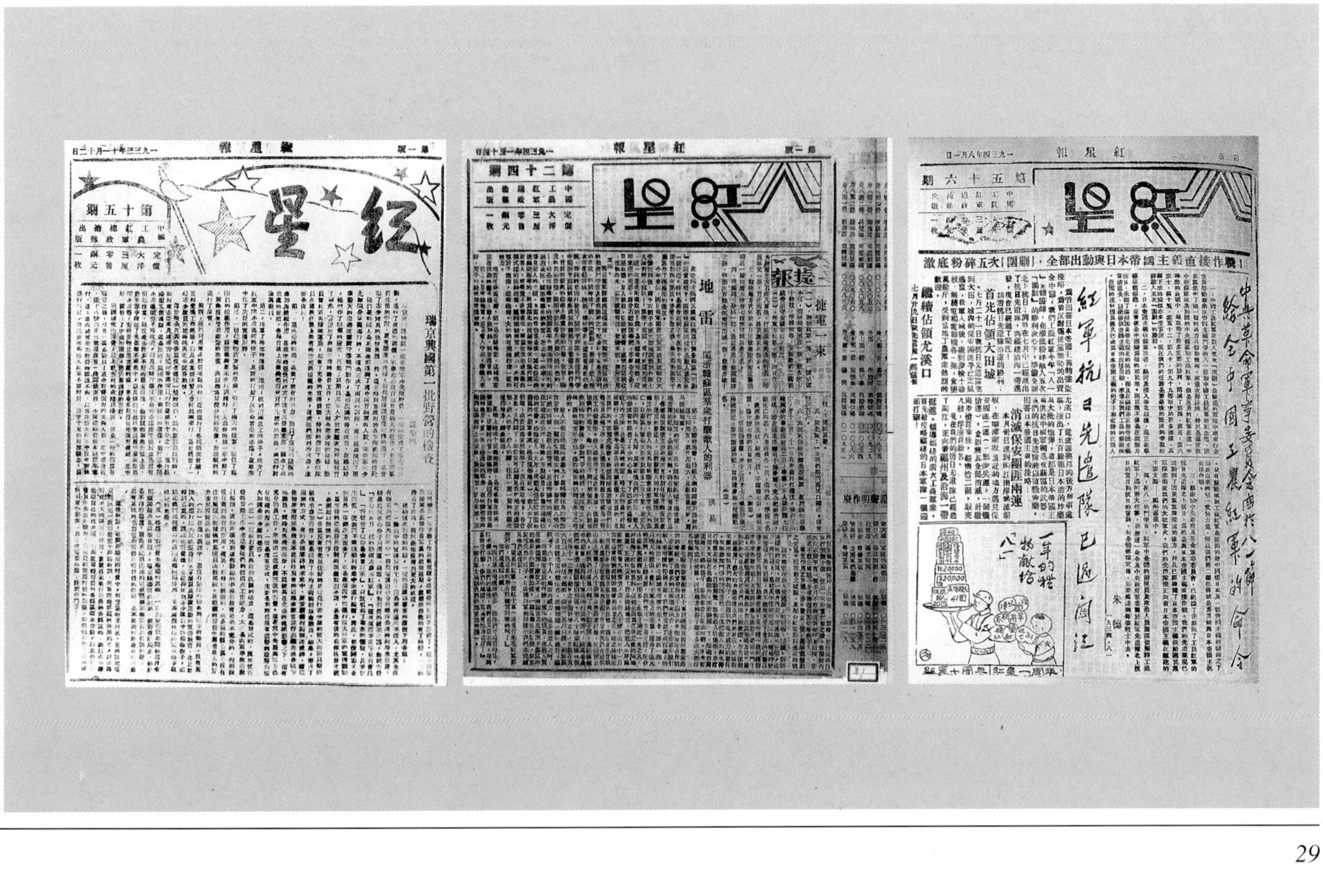

红星

第十五期

紅星

第二十四期

紅星

第五十六期

紅軍抗日先遣隊已過閩江

4

5

6

4. In January, 1935, Deng Xiaoping attended the Enlarged Meeting of the Political Bureau of the Party Central Committee in Zunyi (i.e. the well-known Zunyi Meeting). The photo shows the site of the Zunyi Meeting.

5. The Red Army arrived at Northern Shaanxi after finishing the Long March triumphantly. Deng Xiaoping was in a photo with a group of cadres in Xunyi County. From left: Li Bozhao, Deng Xiaoping, Yang Shangkun, Lu Dingyi, Huang Kecheng, Yang Qiqing, and Luo Ronghuan.

6. In February, 1936, Deng Xiaoping was photographed with some leading cadres of the First Army Group and the Fifteenth Army Group in Chunhua County, Shaanxi Province. From right: Deng Xiaoping, Xu Haidong, Chen Guang, Nie Rongzhen, Cheng Zihua, Yang Shangkun, Luo Ruiqing, and Wang Shoudao.

7

7. In the spring of 1937, Deng Xiaoping, the Director of the Political Department of the First Army Group (first from left, front row) and leaders of the First Army Group Nie Rongzhen (first from the right, front row), Zuo Quan (fourth from the right, front row) and others were taken a photo with democratic personages at Gonghe Town, Gansu province.

Becoming the Deputy Director of the Political Department of the Eighth Route Army Headquarters

1. In early 1938, Deng Xiaoping rode on horse, hurrying to the front-line of the Taihang Mountains.

On August 12, 1937, accompanied by Zhu De, Ye Jianying, and Deng Xiaoping, Zhou Enlai went to Nanjing by air to attend the symposium on the national defense presided over by Chiang Kai-shek. During the meeting, they urged Chiang and Kuomintang to issue a declaration on the cooperation between Kuomintang and the Communist Party and a decision on reorganizing the Red Army. On August 22, the Military Commission of Kuomintang Government in Nanjing issued an official order, deciding that the main forces of the Red Army in northwest China be restructured as the Eighth Route Army (later called the Eighteenth Group Army) of the National Revolutionary Army. On August 25, the Revolutionary Military Commission of the Central Committee of the Chinese Communist Party appointed Ren Bishi and Deng Xiaoping as the Director and Deputy-Director of the Political Department of the Eighth Route Army Headquarters, respectively. After taking the post, Deng Xiaoping was in charge of the daily work of the Political Department. He worked day and night in order to make organizational and mental preparations, in particular the staffing for the whole army. He selected excellent cadres and intellectuals who had just joined the army to set up the political propaganda team and the mass movement work group in the Political Department.

On September 6, 1937, Zhu De, the Commander in Chief, led the Eighth Route Army Headquarters to hold an Anti-Japan mass mobilization rally at Yunyang Town, Sanyuan County, Shaanxi Province, which was presided over by Deng Xiaoping. On the same day, Deng Xiaoping, together with Zhu De, Ren Bishi, and Zuo Quan left Yunyang Town on horseback and passed through several towns, such as Taochi, Dengcheng, and Heyang, finally arriving at Zhichuan Town, Hancheng County on the west bank of the Yellow River on September 14. From this place they crossed the Yellow River by taking a boat to the east bank and reached Wanrong County, Shanxi Province. Later, they went north by taking train at Houma Town, Qu'wo County, Shanxi Province. They arrived in Taiyuan on September 21 and stayed at Taiyuan Office of the Eighth Route Army in Chengcheng Middle School. In northeastern Shangxi, proceeding from organizing the Front General Mobilization Committee of the National Revolutionary War, Deng Xiaoping mobilized the broad mass of people to support the front operations, created base areas, and carried out guerrilla warfare.

In October 1937, Deng Xiaoping, Fu Zhong, Lu Dengyi, and 500-600 men, away from thc main forces, went to the area of Fenyang and Xiaoyi on the foot of the Luliang Mountains to initiate new work in southwestern Shanxi. In December, they moved to southern Shanxi and joined the Eighth Route Army Headquarters at Mamu Village, Hongdong County.

2

2. Deng Xiaoping at the early period of the War of Resistance Against Japan.

3. In September 1937, Deng Xiaoping, the Deputy Director of the Political Department of the Eighth Route Army (third from left), Zhu De (with binoculars), and Ren Bishi (first from left) crossed the Yellow River to its east bank by boat from Zhichuan Town, Hancheng County, Shaanxi Province, and entered the front of Anti-Japanese aggressors in Shanxi Province.

3

4. At the early period of the War of Resistance Against Japan, Deng Xiaoping (second from left) was photographed with several cadres, including Huang Kecheng (first from left) and Fu Zhong (first from right).

5. Get-together of the leading members of the Eighth Route Army Headquarters. From left: Zuo Quan, Peng Dehuai, Zhu De, Peng Xuefeng, Xiao Ke, and Deng Xiaoping.

4

5

Establishing the Anti-Japanese Base Areas in Shanxi, Hebei, Henan, and Other Places

1. In January 1938, Deng Xiaoping became the Political Commissar of the 129th Division of the Eighth Route Army. This photo shows Deng Xiaoping and Liu Bocheng, the Commander of the 129th Division.

In January 1938, the Eighth Route Army Headquarters appointed Deng Xiaoping as the Political Commissar of the 129th Division. On January 18, Deng Xiaoping entered the Taihang Mountains by horseback and arrived at the 129th Division Headquarters at Xihetou Village, Liaoxian (now called Zuo Quan) County, Shanxi Province.

In the first ten days of February, 1938, Deng Xiaoping and Liu Bocheng co-chaired the meeting attended by cadres at and above the regimental level of the Division. During the meeting, they discussed and decided on the work of carrying out guerrilla warfare in the Taihang Mountains and the establishment of base areas. In the Taihang Mountains the 129th Division, under the leadership of Liu Bocheng and Deng Xiaoping, fought and won the battles at Changshengkou, Shentouling, Xiangtangpu, and Changle Village, and basically controlled the Shanxi-Hebei-Henan areas with the Taihang Mountains at the center.

On April 25, 1938, Deng Xiaoping presided over the meeting attended by cadres at and above the level of regimental commander of the 129th Division, during which he transmitted to the participants the directives by the Party Central Committee on extending guerrilla warfare from mountain areas to plain areas and agreed on ways to implement the directives. A decision was made at the meeting that Xu Xiangqian, the Deputy Division Commander, would lead the column of the 129th Division on the eastside of Ping-Han (Beiping-Hankou) railway line and a part of the 115th Division to advance eastward to southern Hebei. At the same time, Deng Xiaoping and Liu Bocheng led the Division Headquarters and 386th Brigade to move towards Xingtai area in western Hebei for the purposes of covering Xu Xiangqian's troops to go eastward. After that, they led the troops to frequently attack and cut off the Ping-Han railway line. They devoted their main efforts to guiding the work in the western and southern Hebei base areas.

On July 5, 1938, Deng Xiaoping arrived at southern Hebei from western Hebei. Together with Xu Xiangqian, Deng Xiaoping specifically guided the reconstruction of local armed forces in that area. He also dispatched a large number of cadres who were Party members to various counties to strengthen the building of political power. In addition, Deng Xiaoping, in Nangong County, southern Hebei, met many times with Lieutenant Commander Evans Fordyce Carlson, the then naval attaché of the United States Embassy to China, explaining to him the principles of the Communist Party on fighting against the Japanese aggressors.

In the late period of August, 1938, Deng Xiaoping was instructed to leave southern Hebei for the Eighth Route Army Headquarters. Before long, he went to Yan'an to attend the Sixth Plenary Session of the Sixth Central Committee of the Chinese Communist Party and presented a report on the field work at the session.

In mid-October, 1938, upon learning that the Japanese troops in North China would launch a massive "mopping-up" operation against the base areas, Deng Xiaoping sent a telegram to Liu Baocheng and Xu Xiangqian from Yan'an. He put forward the following four proposals: the newly organized troops should be trained in rotation; the troops on the eastside to the Ping-Han railway line should make great efforts to raise funds so as to expeditiously provide daily necessities needed by the troops in winter; and the large quantities of food and war industry equipment stored in the eastside to the Ping-Han railway line must be transported to its west side. From the Taihang Mountains, Liu Bocheng drafted a telegram personally and expressed his agreement with Deng's suggestions.

At the end of 1938, after returning from Yan'an to southern Hebei, Deng Xiaoping held a meeting attended by cadres responsible for military and political affairs in the 129th Division. At the meeting, Deng transmitted to the participants the essence of decisions adopted by the Sixth Plenary Session of the Sixth Party Central Committee and elaborated on the principles used to fight the enemy. The meeting decided that the main forces of the Division should move towards southern Hebei by relying on the broad masses of people and rural villages, in order to consolidate the base areas in the plains of southern Hebei and northwestern Shandong.

In January 1939, under the leadership of Deng Xiaoping and Liu Bocheng, the army and the people in southern Hebei, by applying flexible strategy and tactics, fought over 100 battles of a relatively large scale in difficult circumstances. They killed and wounded more than 3,000 Japanese and puppet soldiers, thus shattering the massive "mopping-up" operation by the Japanese troops in an attempt to wipe out the Eighth Route Army troops so as to control the plains in southern Hebei. On March 7, Liu Bocheng and Deng Xiaoping led the main forces of the 129th Division back to the Taihang Mountains.

In August 1939, Deng Xiaoping, upon instruction, went to Yan'an to attend the enlarged meeting of the Political Bureau of the Party Central Committee. In Yan'an, Deng Xiaoping married Zhuo Lin. In early September, Deng Xiaoping and his wife went back to the Taihang Mountains.

On August 12, 1940, Liu Bocheng and Deng Xiaoping led 38 regiments to participate in the world-renowned "Hundred Regiments Offensive," a major military operation that shook the whole country. They fought over 500 large and small battles, killing over 8,000 Japanese and puppet soldiers in total.

2

2. In the spring of 1938, Deng Xiaoping giving a mobilization speech to soldiers in Licheng, Shanxi.

3. Under the direct leadership of the Eighth Route Army Headquarters, the 129th Division marched towards the area of the Taihang Mountains and created the anti-Japan base area behind the enemy lines with the Taihang Mountains as the center. The photo shows that in 1938, Deng Xiaoping (left), the Political Commissar of the 129th Division, Zhu De (right), the Commander in Chief of the Eighth Route Army, and Liu Bocheng, the Commander of the 129th Division were discussing the operation plans.

3

4. In the spring of 1938, Deng Xiaoping (center) making a report at the cadres' meeting of the 129th Division.

5. Together with the main leaders of the 129th Division. From left: Li Da, the Chief of Staff, Deng Xiaoping, the Political Commissar, Liu Bocheng, the Commander, and Cai Shufan, the Director of the Political Department.

6. A photo of some leaders from the Party Central Committee and the Eighth Route Army Headquarters was taken at Yan'an airport. From left: Cheng Zihua, Guan Xiangying, Xiao Ke, Luo Ronghuan, Teng Daiyuan, Deng Xiaoping, Zhu De, Zhou Enlai, Peng Dehuai, He Long, and Xu Haidong.

7. A group photo was taken in Yan'an in November 1938. From left: Deng Xiaoping, Tan Zheng, Chen Yun, Lin Biao, Luo Ronghuan, Luo Ruiqing, Wang Jiaxiang, Yang Shangkun, Teng Daiyuan, He Long, and Li Fuchun.

4

5

6

7

8

8. In December 1938, Deng Xiaoping (left) together with Zhang Wenbin (Zhang Chunqing) in Xi'an.

9. In early September 1939, Deng Xiaoping (first from right) and Zhuo Lin (second from right), Kong Yuan (second from left), and Xu Ming held wedding ceremony in Yan'an. A few days later, Deng Xiaoping and Zhuo Lin hurried to the front of the Taihang Mountains.

10. In winter of 1939, Deng Xiaoping (left) was with Li Tianyou.

9

10

11

11. In 1939, Mao Zedong (sixth from right of those standing) was photographed with some cadres of the Eighth Route Army in Yan'an (third from left at front is Deng Xiaoping).

12. In the spring of 1940, Nie Rongzhen and Lu Zhengcao, leaders from Shanxi-Chahaer-Hebei Military Region, and Liu Bocheng and Deng Xiaoping exchanged their experiences of work against the "mopping-up" operation in their respective regions. The photo shows Deng Xiaoping, Zhu De, Nie Rongzhen, and others at Tongyu Town, southeastern Shanxi.

12

13

13. In 1940, Deng Xiaoping (second from right at front), Liu Bocheng (third from right), Zhu De (third from left), and Nie Rongzhen (second from left) were at Tongyu Town, southeastern Shanxi.

14

15

14. In August 1940, the Eighth Route Army Headquarters led its troops and launched the "Hundred Regiments Offensive" against the Japanese invading troops stationed in North China. Just before the "Offensive," there was a get-together of the leaders from the Party, government, and army of Shanxi-Hebei-Henan anti-Japan base areas. From left: Deng Xiaoping, Li Da, Cai Shufan, Yang Xiufeng, and Liu Bocheng.

15. Deng Xiaoping (left), Liu Bocheng (right), and Cai Shufan were at Wuxiang County, Shanxi.

16. After the "Hundred Regiments Offensive," the 129th Division held a summing-up meeting, during which Deng Xiaoping (sitting on the right) and Liu Bocheng summarized the experiences and lessons learned from the operations.

17. At the end of 1940, Deng Xiaoping (right), Liu Bocheng (center), and Li Da.

16

17

18

19

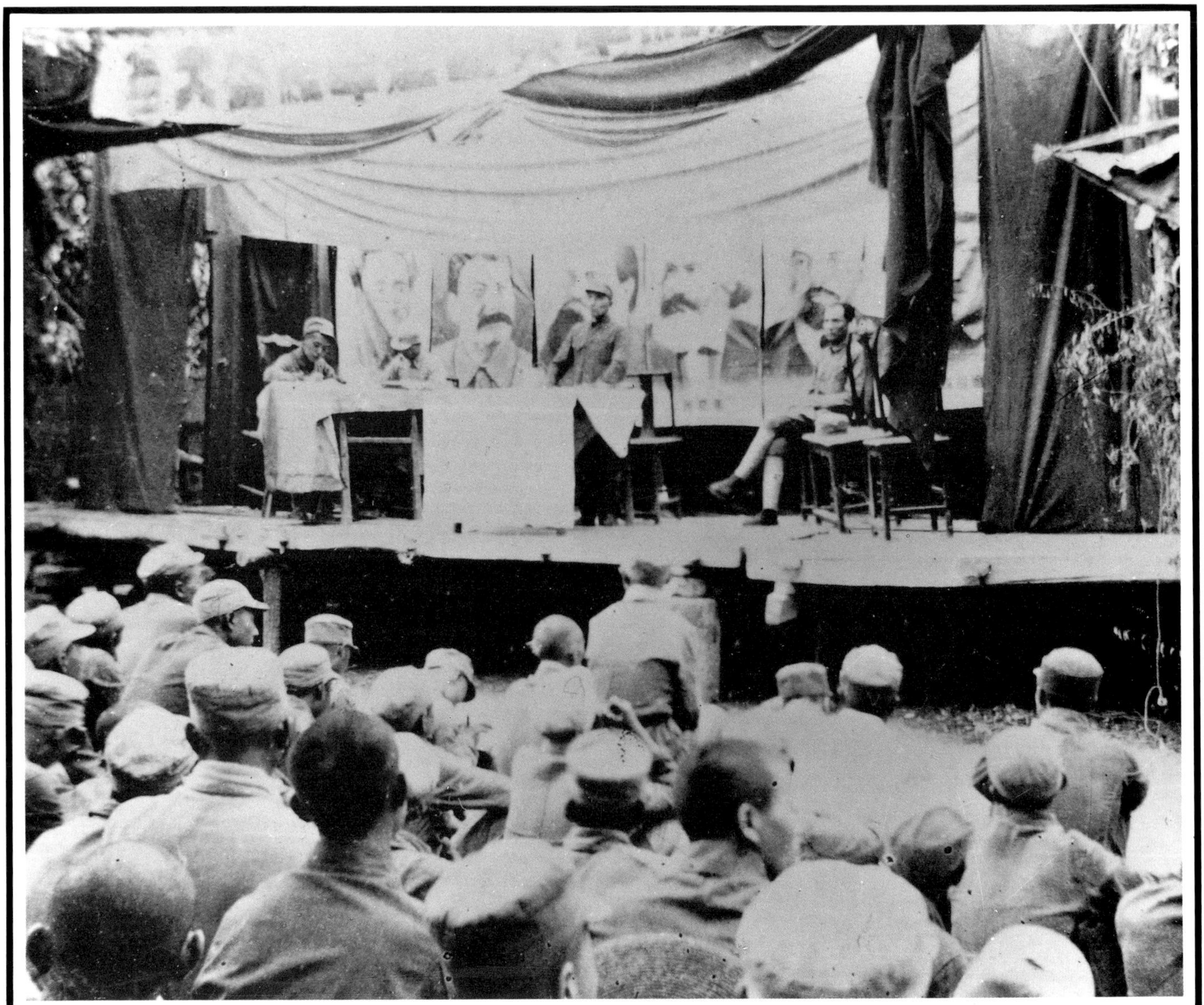

20

18. In 1942, Deng Xiaoping and others standing on the reviewing stand of the sports meet organized by the 129th Division. From left: Teng Daiyuan, Cai Shufan, Deng Xiaoping, Li Da, and Peng Dehuai.

19. In 1941, Deng Xiaoping making a speech at the meeting held by the 129th Division of the Eighth Route Army to elect senators of the Shanxi-Hebei-Henan Consultative Council.

20. The leaders of the 129th Division attended the gala of the new year collective greetings. From left: Liu Bocheng, Deng Xiaoping, Cai Shufan, Li Da, and Wang Shusheng.

21

21. On October 10, 1942, Deng Xiaoping (third from left at front row of those standing on the high platform) was photographed with the entire staff of the Command of the Eighth Route Army Headquarters in front of the tomb of General Zuo Quan.

22. During the War of Resistance Against Japan, Deng Xiaoping showed great concern for the cultural construction of the army. These are the "Battlefield Pictorials" published at that time and the inscriptions written by Deng Xiaoping for the pictorial.

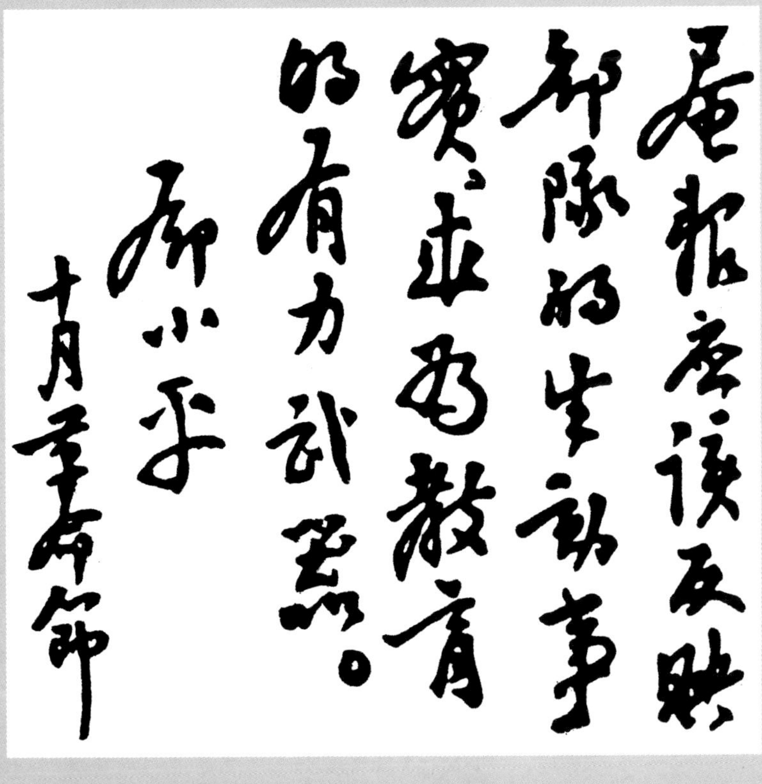

22

23

23. Deng Xiao Peng and his son.

Taking the Important Responsibility to Lead the Anti-Japanese Base Areas in North China

1. Taking the Important Responsibility to Lead the Anti-Japanese Base Areas in North China.

After the "Hundred Regiments Offensive," the anti-Japanese base areas behind the enemy lines in North China entered into an unprecedented difficult and hard period. In view of the existing situation, Deng Xiaoping wrote the following articles entitled "A Number of Issues Concerning the Building of Military Region, The Party, and Anti-Japanese Democratic Political Power and Opposing Indifference and Apathy, Reversing the Grave Situation in the Taihang Mountains." They were published in magazines, such as *The Battlefront* and *The Party's Life*, issued between March and April of 1941.

In January 1942, Deng Xiaoping and Liu Bocheng held a mobilization meeting for streamlining the military and administrative structure. A decision was made at the meeting to downsize the administrative offices, reinforce the combating companies, and strengthen the local armed forces. On September 7, Mao Zedong wrote the editorial entitled "A Very Important Policy" for the *Liberation Daily* published in Yan'an, in which he praised the leading comrades of Shanxi-Hebei-Shandong-Henan Border Region for seizing their work tightly and setting a good example for streamlining the military and administrative structure.

From March 19 to June 24, 1942, Deng Xiaoping led a regiment by himself to go to Yuebei, Yuenan, and Zhongtiao Mountain (Shanxi-Henan Anti-Japanese Base Area) to examine and assign work there.

In September 1942, the Party Central Committee decided to set up Taihang Sub-bureau of North China Bureau of the Party Central Committee and appointed Deng Xiaoping as its Secretary so as to integrate the leadership the four Party district committees of Shanxi-Hebei-Henan, Southern Hebei, Taiyue, and Zhongtiao.

Between January and February 1943, Taihang Sub-bureau of North China Bureau of the Party Central Committee held a meeting of high-ranking cadres at Wencun Village, Shexian County, Henan (now belonged to Hebei Province), discussing the issues of restoration and further development of Shanxi-Hebei-Shandong-Henan anti-Japanese base areas. Deng Xiaoping presided over the meeting and delivered a report on the summary of the struggle against the enemy in the past five years, as well as principles of the struggle against the enemy in the future.

In his article entitled "The Economic Construction in the Taihang District," published in the *Liberation Daily* of July 2, 1943, Deng Xiaoping expounded the significance of the struggle in the economic field carried out behind the enemy lines and the relationship between the struggle in the economic field and economic construction.

On September 21, 1943, Deng Xiaoping chaired the meeting for the economic production of the entire Shanxi-Hebei-Shandong-Henan region and made a report entitled "Striving for Production and Tiding Over Difficulties to Win Victory" at the meeting. After the meeting, the army and the people in base areas unfolded a vigorous mass campaign for autumn cultivation and opening up virgin soil. Deng Xiaoping practiced what he advocated by leasing two *mu* public paddy fields, together with Zhang Jichun and others. They wrote a so-called "military pledge," promising to pay in the following year the lease fee and other expenses in accordance with the stipulations.

Between September and October 1943, after Peng Dehuai, Liu Bocheng, and others left the Taihang Mountains successively for Yan'an to participate in the rectification movement, Deng Xiaoping became the Acting Secretary of North China Bureau of the Party Central Committee and was in charge of the work of the Eighth Route Army Headquarters. He thus took the important responsibility to lead the anti-Japanese base areas in North China.

In January 1944, on behalf of the North China Bureau of the Party Central Committee, Deng Xiaoping issued an instruction "On the Guiding Principles for the Work of 1944," in which he pointed out that the central tasks for all of North China were to intensify the struggle against the enemy, make great efforts for production, and carry out the rectification movement so as to make preparations for counteroffensive.

In July 1944, Deng Xiaoping summoned Pi Dingjun and Xu Zirong, the Commander and the Political Commissar of the 5th Sub-region of Taihang Military Region, respectively, and transmitted to them the instructions from the Party Central Committee. They were ordered to advance towards the areas behind the enemy lines in Henan. He proposed the establishment of the Western Henan Anti-Japanese Detachment of the Eighth Route Army and asked them to cross the Yellow River from the north bank immediately so as to set up an Anti-Japanese base area in western Henan.

At the end of June 1945, Deng Xiaoping, after being elected as a member of the Party Seventh Central Committee, left the Taihang Mountains for Yan'an to attend the First Plenary Session of the Party Seventh Central Committee. In Yan'an, he often discussed with Liu Bocheng how to carry out the struggle in Shanxi-Hebei-Shandong-Henan Border Regions for seizing and defending the fruits of the victory in the War of Resistance Against Japan.

On August 15, 1945, the Japanese government proclaimed its unconditional surrender. Deng Xiaoping, Liu Bocheng, and Teng Daiyuan sent telegrams from Yan'an to various military regions in Shanxi-Hebei-Shandong-Henan and instructed them to recover the lost territory quickly and strengthen the corps of the main forces immediately in order to counterattack the offensive from the north by the Kuomintang troops along the Ping-Han and Tong-Pu (Datong-Pukou) railway lines.

On August 20, 1945, the Party Central Committee decided to set up Shanxi-Hebei-Shandong-Henan Bureau of the Central Committee and Shanxi-Hebei-Shandong-Henan Military Region, and appointed Deng Xiaoping as the Secretary of the Bureau and the Political Commissar of the Military Region. So far, the Shanxi-Hebei-Shandong-Henan liberated areas based on and developed from Taihang Mountains Anti-Japanese base areas had a population of 25 million people, 300,000 army men, and 400,000 people's militia.

2

2. In August 1945, Deng Xiaoping became the Secretary of Shanxi-Hebei-Shandong-Henan Bureau of the Party Central Committee, and concurrently the Political Commissar of Shanxi-Hebei-Shandong-Henan Military Region.

3. In 1945, the Commander of Shanxi-Hebei-Shandong-Henan Military Region Liu Bocheng (center), the Political Commissar Deng Xiaoping (left), and the Deputy Commander Teng Daiyuan were together.

3

Defending the Fruits of Victory of the War of Resistance Against Japan & Smashing Full-scale Offensive Launched by the Kuomintang Troops

1. Deng Xiaoping at early period in the War of Liberation.

On August 25, 1945, Deng Xiaoping, Liu Bocheng, and others flew from Yan'an to the Taihang Mountains in a U.S-made cargo plane.

On August 28, 1945, in accordance with the instructions by the Central Military Commission on assembling the superior forces in Taihang and Taiyue in order to first annihilate Yan Xishan's puppet troops who entered Changzhi, Liu Bocheng and Deng Xiaoping held a meeting at Chi'an Village, Shexian County, to discuss how to deploy troops for the Shangdang Campaign.

On September 10, 1945, Liu Bocheng and Deng Xiaoping commanded armed forces of over 31,000 men to wage the Shangdang Campaign, and destroyed Yan Xishan's 13 divisions with 35,000 men in total belonging to the Second Combat Zone of Kuomintang. This was the first major battle between Kuomintang and the Communist Party after the victory of the War of Resistance Against Japan. This victory dealt a head-on blow to the Kuomintang troops who invaded the liberated areas, and it also encouraged the fighting will of the army and the people and provided a strong support for Mao Zedong in his negotiations with Chiang Kai-shek in Chongqing.

In mid-October 1945, Liu Bocheng and Deng Xiaoping directed more than 60,000 soldiers from both the main forces and local armed forces to carry on the Ping-Han Campaign (the Handan Campaign). They killed and wounded over 3,000 enemy soldiers and captured Ma Fawu, the Deputy Commander of the Kuomintang's 11th Combat Zone, and concurrently the Commander of the 40th Army, as well as some 23,000 soldiers in total. They persuaded Gao Shuxun, the Commander of the newly organized 8th Army, to lead more than 10,000 soldiers to revolt, and thus won the second major battle between Kuomintang and the Communist Party after the victory of the War of Resistance Against Japan.

In November 1945, Deng Xiaoping presided over the plenary session of the Shanxi-Hebei-Shandong-Henan Bureau of the Party Central Committee at Fengfeng coal mine, in a suburb of Handan City to elaborate on the work of the whole region. At the meeting,

Deng Xiaoping seriously criticized some comrades who were demoralized, weary of war, and claimed credit and put on airs. He called on the army and people in the region to get a full understanding of Chiang Kai-shek's counterrevolutionary nature, to strive to surmount all kinds of difficulties, and make full preparations for a protracted civil war.

Between April and May, 1946, Shanxi-Hebei-Shandong-Henan Military Region issued the following directives jointly signed by Liu Bocheng and Deng Xiaoping: "The Directives on Making Preparations for the Civil War," "The Guiding Principles on Armed Struggle for Shanxi-Hebei-Shandong-Henan Military Region," and "The Directives on How to Deal with a Full-scale Civil War and How to Intensify the Preparation." They demanded the army and the people in the region heighten their vigilance, make good use of the warless period to grasp tightly the training of soldiers and carry out the movement of reduction of rent for land and of interest on loans, as well as the movement of great production.

In June 1946, Chiang Kai-shek openly tore up the Agreement of October 10 and the Armistice Agreement into pieces, and launched an all-round civil war by besieging the Central Plains liberated areas as its starting point. On June 28, the main forces of Shanxi-Hebei-Shandong-Henan Field Army held a mass rally for carrying out patriotic self-defense operations at Matou Town in the suburb south of Handan City. Deng Xiaoping attended the meeting and made a speech.

At the end of July 1946, Liu Bocheng and Deng Xiaoping presided over a meeting on military affairs at Bagongqiao, Puyang. A decision was made at the meeting that the main forces should launch a full-scale attack on sections between Xuzhou and Kaifeng of the Long-Hai railway line where the enemy's defense was relatively weak, so as to support by coordinated action the Central Plains Field Army to break out of an encirclement and take concerted action with Jiangsu-Anhui troops in the military operations. At the same time, some cadres and soldiers were selected to organize a command post of the Field Army led by Liu Bocheng and Deng Xiaoping themselves, and moved from Handan towards the Hebei-Shandong-Henan frontline.

On August 4, 1946, Liu Bocheng and Deng Xiaoping issued Basic Orders for the Long-Hai Campaign at Heze, Shandong Province. They commanded three columns of the main forces to launch a fierce attack upon the enemy stationed along 100-kilometer sections between the Xuzhou and Kaifeng Long-Hai railway line and wiped out 16,000 enemy soldiers.

On August 31, 1946, Liu Bocheng and Deng Xiaoping issued an order for the Dingtao Campaign to the troops, which later completely annihilated the reorganized 3rd Division of Kuomintang in the area west of Dingdao. In this campaign, four brigades with over 17,000 enemy soldiers were wiped out.

On September 29, 1946, Liu Bocheng and Deng Xiaoping issued an order for the Juye Campaign. This campaign lasted one month, i.e. from September 29 to October 30, and more than 14,000 enemy soldiers were annihilated.

On November 12, 1946, Liu Bocheng and Deng Xiaoping issued an order for the Huaxian Campaign. 12,000 enemy soldiers were annihilated in this campaign, which lasted from November 15 to November 22.

On December 20, 1946, Liu Bocheng and Deng Xiaoping issued an order for the Juye-Jinxiang-Yutai Campaign. In this campaign, three and half brigades of the Kuomintang regular army, together with local armed forces totaling over 16,000 enemy soldiers were wiped out.

On January 24, 1947, in order to cooperate with the East China Field Army in carrying out the Laiwu Campaign, Liu Bocheng and Deng Xiaoping divided their troops into the south and north army groups and launched an offensive on the areas south and north of the Long-Hai railway line. This was also called "attacking the Long-Hai railway line for the second time." Led by Deng Xiaoping, the south army group captured the cities of Tuocheng, Haozhou, and Luyi one after another. As of February 11, the Filed Army led by Liu Bocheng and Deng Xiaoping had annihilated more than 16,000 enemy soldiers in total.

On March 19, 1947, Liu Bocheng and Deng Xiaoping issued an order for the Yubei (northern Henan) Campaign. In this campaign, carried out from March 22 to May 25, over 45,000 enemy soldiers in total were wiped out. At the same time, the 4th Column under Shanxi-Hebei-Shandong-Henan Military Region and the troops from Taiyue Military Region annihilated more than 18,000 enemy soldiers in a counteroffensive operation in southern Shanxi. The counteroffensive operations carried out in Northern Henan and Southern Shanxi strongly supported the Liberation Army fighting on the interior line in Northern Shaanxi and Shandong battlefields, and also created favorable conditions for the offensive to be launched later in the Central Plains.

On June 21, 1947, at the meeting of cadres at and above the level of battalion commander from teams directly under the Field Army, Deng Xiaoping made a mobilization speech on the strategic counteroffensive and a report to answer the questions concerning the current situation and tasks. He analyzed in detail the situation in the second year of the War of Liberation, and elaborated thoroughly on the necessity of a strategic counteroffensive.

On June 22, 1947, Liu Bocheng and Deng Xiaoping issued an order for the Western-Southern-Shandong Campaign. On the night of June 30, led by Liu Bocheng and Deng Xiaoping, over 100,000 soldiers of the main forces of the Field Army simultaneously broke through the natural barrier of the Yellow River on the 150-kilometer long section from Zhangqiu Town to Linpuji. This was the prelude to the strategic counteroffensive launched by the People's Liberation Army. The army, under the leadership of Liu Bocheng and Deng Xiaoping, wiped out nine and a half brigades of the Kuomintang regular army and four divisions headquarters, as well as killing, wounding, and capturing over 60,000 enemy soldiers in this Campaign.

2. On August 26, 1945, Deng Xiaoping, Liu Bocheng, and others flew from Yan'an to the front of the Taihang Mountains. This photo was taken at the airport. From left, back row: Chen Yi, Deng Xiaoping, Liu Bocheng, Teng Daiyuan, Xiao Jinguang, Chen Geng. Li Fuchun (first from right, front row) and Nie Rongzhen (second from right, front row).

3. The Shangdang Campaign was a major victory. The photo shows our army attacking the wall and the pass of Tunliu city.

2

3

4

4. **In the Handan Campaign, our army captured Ma Fawu alive, the Deputy Commander of the Kuomintang's 11th Combat Zone, as well as his troops, totaling more than 23,000 soldiers. This group photo was taken when Deng Xiaoping (first from left), Liu Bocheng, and Bo Yibo sent Ma Fawu (in unlined long gown) in courtesy back to Xinxiang.**

5. **In 1946, Deng Xiaoping (center, front row) was photographed with members of the military mediation group in Handan.**

6. **The calligraphy by Deng Xiaoping in 1946, "Uphold independence, peace and democracy, oppose treachery, civil war and dictatorship."**

6

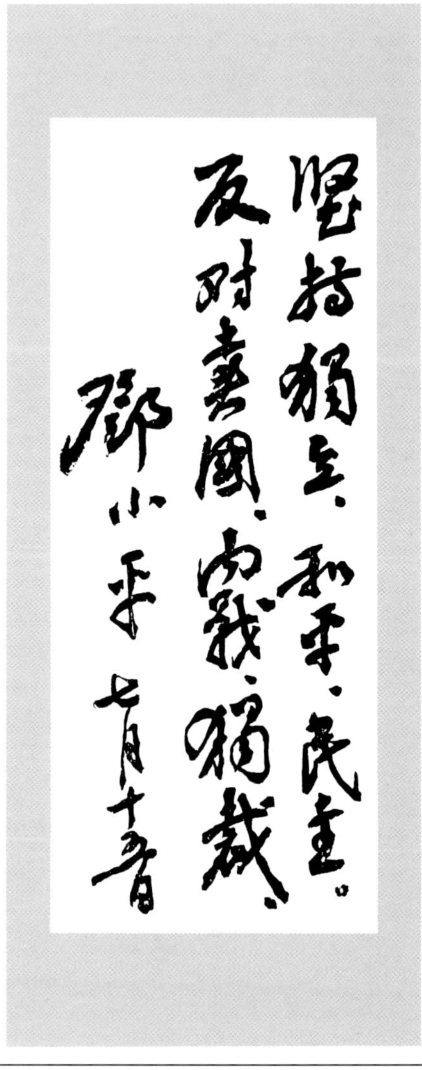

5

7

8

9

7. Deng Xiaoping (second from right) and Liu Bocheng reviewed the troops before the military operations.

8. In August 1946, the Long-Hai Campaign started. The photo shows that Deng Xiaoping (first from left), Liu Bocheng, and Bo Yibo were at the mobilization rally before the military operations.

9. In September 1946, Deng Xiaoping and Liu Bocheng organized and commanded the Dingtao Campaign. The photo shows the machine-gun position of our army in the Dayanghu battle.

10

10. In November 1946, after the Huaxian Campaign, Deng Xiaoping (first from left, back row) and Liu Bocheng met with Yang Xianming (first from right), the Commander of the 104th Brigade of Kuomintang army, and others captured by our army.

11. On the night of June 30, led by Liu Bocheng and Deng Xiaoping, over 100,000 soldiers of the main forces of the Shanxi-Hebei-Shandong-Henan Field Army suddenly broke through the natural barrier of the Yellow River and marched towards southern and western Shandong. This was the prelude to the strategic counteroffensive launched by the People's Liberation Army.

11

Advancing Hundreds of Miles towards the Dabie Mountains & Re-establishing the Base Areas in the Central Plains

1. On August 27, 1947, the main forces of the army, led by Liu Bocheng and Deng Xiaoping, succeeded in arriving at the foot of the Dabie Mountains.

On August 2, 1947, Liu Bocheng and Deng Xiaoping called together the leaders of military and political affairs of various columns to have a meeting, and discussed and assigned the operations moving towards the south. On August 6, another meeting, attended by cadres at and above the levels of department and section chief in the Command, was presided over by Liu Bocheng and Deng Xiaoping at the war room in the Headquarters. At the meeting, a decision was adopted that the army take a strategic leap at once and advance towards the Dabie Mountains.

On August 7, 1947, Liu Bocheng and Deng Xiaoping led 130,000 soldiers of the main forces to take a sudden action; they crossed the Long-Hai railway line from the areas between Minquan and Shangqiu, as well as Yucheng in southwestern Shandong. By this action, the strategic advancement hundreds of miles towards the Dabie Mountains began. After more than 20 days of military operations without any support from the rear, the troops commanded by Liu Bocheng and Deng Xiaoping crossed such natural barriers as the Wuohe River, the Huanghe River (Yellow River) Inundated Area, the Shahe River, the Honghe River, the Ruhe River, and the Huaihe River one after another. They finally succeeded in arriving at Huangchuan and Gushi areas located at the foot of the Dabie Mountains on August 27.

On August 31, 1947, Liu Bocheng and Deng Xiaoping held a meeting at Beixiangdian, Guangshan County, which was attended by the cadres at and above the level of company commander directly under the Field Army. They called on all the officers and men to establish the Dabie Mountains base areas wholeheartedly and without turning back. At the meeting, Deng Xiaoping delivered a report on the current situation and tasks before us.

On September 27, 1947, at the meeting attended by the cadres at and above the level of brigade commander at Wangdawan, northwest to Shangcheng, Henan Province, Liu Bocheng and Deng Xiaoping further expounded the strategic significance of establishing the Dabie Mountains base areas. They emphasized that the basic conditions for the army to stand firm in the Dabie Mountains were to strengthen the confidence, oppose the Right-deviationist thinking, and eliminate acts of indiscipline. To the end of September, the army led by Liu Bocheng and Deng Xiaoping captured 23 county seats successively, such as Macheng, Yun'an, Huang'an, Yuexi, and Guangji. These actions made a breakthrough for re-establishing the base areas and achieved initial results to realize the strategic plan made by the Central Military Commission and Mao Zedong on bringing the war into the zones controlled by Kuomintang.

At the end of November 1947, 14 divisions plus 33 brigades of Kuomintang army launched an all-out seige on the Dabie Mountains. According to the instructions from the Central Military Commission, Liu Bocheng and Deng Xiaoping decided to adopt the strategy of persevering to the end on the interior line and dividing troops to the outer line, thus cooperating from both lines and trying to locate and wipe out the vulnerable enemy troops. At the same time, another decision was also made to set up the Front and Rear Command Posts of the Field Army. Deng Xiaoping, Li Xiannian, and Li Da led the Front Command Post to remain in the Dabie Mountains to direct fighting on the interior line; Liu Bocheng and Zhang Jichun commanded the Rear Command Post to cross the Huaihe River from the south side to fight on the outer line.

In mid-December 1947, the enemy forces had an absolute advantage over us, and they were so concentrated and close to each other that they could easily launch an attack. Furthermore, the inner land of the Dabie Mountains was surrounded by high mountains and covered with narrow paths, and there was little room to maneuver. In consideration of the above, Deng Xiaoping and others decided to adopt a flexible tactic of dispersing at one time and concentrating at other times our forces to wipe out the enemy troops in many back-and-forth mobile operations. After nearly two months of arduous military operations, the army forces remained in the Dabie Mountains annihilated 15,000 enemy soldiers in total, occupied more than a dozen county seats successively, such as Taihu, Yingshan, Qianshan, and Huangmei, and won an important victory fighting on the interior line.

On February 22, 1948, on behalf of the Central Plains Bureau of the Party Central Committee, Deng Xiaoping signed and issued a directive on carrying out the guerrilla warfare in the Dabie Mountains. It requested the troops of the Military Region and the local armed forces to hang on by self-reliance in this strategic area of the Dabie Mountains, carry out the mass guerrilla war, and fight against and annihilate the scattered enemy troops.

On February 24, 1948, led by Deng Xiaoping, the Front Command Post of the Field Army left the Dabie Mountains and crossed the Huaihe River to its north side. They arrived at Weizhai, south of Linquan County, Anhui Province, to join the Rear Command Post of the Field Army led by Liu Bocheng. After that, Liu Bocheng and Deng Xiaoping deployed the main forces of the Field Army from the Dabie Mountains to the area north of the Huaihe River and in Western Henan for assembling, training, and consolidation. They later joined the forces of Corps led by Chen Geng and Xie Fuzhi and Corps led by Chen Shiqu and Tang Liang (the latter belonged to the Field Army led by Chen Yi), getting prepared to find an opportunity to destroy the enemy.

On March 7, 1948, Liu Bocheng and Deng Xiaoping led their troops to start the Luoyang Campaign and wiped out approximately 20,000 enemy soldiers.

In mid-April 1948, after moving to the Guodian Town, east to Yexian County in Western Henan, the Central Plains Bureau of the Party Central Committee and the Command Post of the Field Army, led by Liu Bocheng and Deng Xiaoping, made good use of this relatively stable environment and seized the time to train, consolidate, and replenish the armed forces.

On April 25, 1948, at the joint meeting of the Front and the Rear Committees of Henan-Shaanxi-Hubei held at Lushan, Henan Province, Deng Xiaoping delivered a report on the victorious situation of marching towards the central plains and the future policies and strategies.

From May 2 to 17, 1948, the army led by Liu Bocheng and Deng Xiaoping launched the Yuanxi Campaign, wiped out 21,000 enemy soldiers, and recaptured more than 10 county seats and towns in the Yuanxi area.

On May 9, 1948, in order to strengthen the leadership of the Central Plains Bureau, the Party Central Committee appointed Deng Xiaoping as its First Secretary, Chen Yi the Second Secretary, Deng Zihui the Third Secretary, and Liu Bocheng, Li Xiannian, Su Yu, Song Renqiong, Chen Geng, Zhang Jichun, Tan Zhenlin, and Li Da as its members. At the same time, the Party Central Committee decided to set up the Central Plains Military Region and renamed the southward crusade Field Army of Shanxi-Hebei-Shandong-Henan (including the Corps led by Chen Geng and Xie Fuzhi) as the Central Plains Field Army, appointed Liu Bocheng as the Commander of the Central Plains Military Region, and the Central Plains Field Army, with Deng Xiaoping as their Political Commissar and Chen Yi as their First Deputy-Commander.

In late May of 1948, in accordance with the instructions from the Central Military Commission, Liu Bocheng and Deng Xiaoping decided to launch the Wandong Campaign. More than 10,000 enemy soldiers were wiped out during this campaign lasted from May 25 to June 3.

From mid-June to mid-July 1948, Liu Bocheng and Deng Xiaoping took three intercepting actions, first against the enemy at Xiping area along the south section of Ping-Han railway line so as to coordinate the East China Field Army for its Kaifeng Campaign and Sui-Qi (Suixian County and Qixian County) Campaign in eastern Henan. Then, they launched the Laoxiang Campaign, annihilated over 20,000 enemy soldiers, and liberated Laohekou, Xiangyang, and Fancheng.

2

2. The southward crusade troops were wading across the Huaihe River.

3. On August 31, 1947, Deng Xiaoping made a speech at the meeting of cadres held at Beixiangdian, Guangshan County, in the Dabie Mountains.

3

4

4. On March 15, 1948, Deng Xiaoping made a report on the work of consolidating the Party organization at the meeting of cadres from the Central Plains Bureau of the Party Central Committee.

5. Deng Xiaoping, looking at picture exhibition reflecting the life of army officers and men.

6. In 1948, the leaders of the Central Plains Bureau of the Party Central Committee and the Central Military Region were together. From right: Deng Xiaoping, Li Da, Li Xuefeng, Zhang Jichun, Liu Bocheng, and Chen Yi.

5

6

7

7. In May 1948, the Central Plains Field Army joined forces with the East China Field Army in the Central Plains. Deng Xiaoping (first from right) and Liu Bocheng meeting with members of the delegation sent to the fields to convey greetings and appreciation from the East China Field Army.

8. In May 1948, Deng Xiaoping (first from left), Liu Bocheng, and Li Da having a dinner party with the members of the delegation sent to the fields to convey greetings and appreciation from the East China Field Army.

8

9. On July 31, 1948, in Baofeng, Henan Province, the Central Plains Bureau of the Party Central Committee and the Central Plains Military Region held a meeting attended by cadres at and above the level of regimental commander and a meeting of consolidation of the army with a new approach. The photo shows Deng Xiaoping chatting with Chen Yi and others during the meetings.

9

The Secretary of the General Front Committee at Frontline of the Huai-Hai Campaign

1. On January 10, 1949, the Huai-Hai Campaign ended victoriously.

At the end of August 1948, Deng Xiaoping went to Xibaipo to attend the enlarged meeting of the Political Bureau of the Party Central Committee.

On October 11, 1948, in order to coordinate the military operation by the East China Field Army to defeat the enemy corps led by Huang Botao at the area east of Xuzhou, Liu Bocheng, Deng Xiaoping, and Chen Yi decided after deliberation that Deng Xiaoping and Chen Yi should lead the 1st, 3rd, 4th, and 9th Columns under the Central Plains Field Army to advance north towards Zhengzhou to attack and attract, at the same time, a portion of the enemy troops from Sun Yuanliang's Corps and Qiu Qingquan's Corps back to support Huang Botao's Corps; while Liu Bocheng, Deng Zihui, and Li Da lead the 2nd and 6th Columns under the Central Plains Field Army and the forces from the Military Regions to remain in western Henan to pin down the enemy forces of Zhang Gan's Corps and Huang Wei's Corps. From October 19 to 24, the armed forces led by Deng Xiaoping and Chen Yi captured Zhengzhou, Kaifeng, and other cities successively.

On November 10, 1948, Liu Bocheng rushed to Tuocheng, Henan Province, from the western part of that province to join with Deng Xiaoping and Chen Yi. After repeated deliberations, they issued an operation order to attack and occupy Suxian County so as to cut off the connections of enemy forces between Xuzhou and Bengbu.

On November 16, 1948, in order to strengthen the unified leadership of the Liberation Army at the Huai-Hai front, the Central Military Commission decided to establish the General Front Committee consisting of Liu Bocheng, Chen Yi, Deng Xiaoping, Su Yu, and Tan Zhenlin. Deng Xiaoping was appointed as its Secretary, and Liu Bocheng, Chen Yi, and Deng Xiaoping as members of its Standing Committee.

On November 19, 1948, after analyzing and studying the battlefield situation on both south and north lines, the General Front Committee, with Deng Xiaoping as its Secretary, sent two telegrams consecutively to the Central Military Commission. They suggested that the second phase operation of the Huai-Hai Campaign should be focused on the south line and let the Central Plains Field Army attack Huang Wei's Corps and the East China Field Army attack Li Yannian's Corps. This proposal was accepted by the Central Military Commission and endorsed by the East China Field Army.

On November 22, 1948, the main forces of the East China Field Army wiped out Huang Botao's Corps at the north line. In light of the situation that the enemy troops of Li Yannian's Corps and Liu Ruming's Corps were slow in action, while Huang Wei's Corps, an isolated force, advanced recklessly, the General Front Committee, in its telegram sent to the Central Military Commission on the late night of November 23, suggested that the Field Army should first attack Huang's Corps. The Central Military Commission and Mao Zedong once again accepted the proposal put forward by the General Front Committee. In its reply message to the General Front Committee and the East China Field Army on the afternoon of November 24, the Central Military Commission stressed the following three points: (1) completely agreed with the proposal to attack Huang Wei first; (2) expected that the East China Field Army abide by the troop deployment decisions by Liu Bocheng, Deng Xiaoping, and Chen Yi, and dispatch necessary forces to participate in the military action against Huang Wei; (3) in case of emergency, Liu Bocheng, Deng Xiaoping, and Chen Yi could make decisions, whenever appropriate, without asking for instructions.

On December 15, 1948, the second-phase operation of the Huai-Hai Campaign ended victoriously. About 120,000 enemy soldiers, including one Corps Headquarters, four Army Headquarters, 11 divisions, and one high-speed column were wiped out. At the same time, the East China Field Army annihilated 12,000 enemy soldiers in the intercepting operation against two corps led by Li Yannian and Liu Ruming.

On December 16, 1948, Liu Bocheng, Chen Yi, and Deng Xiaoping arrived at Caiwa Village, where the Command Post of the East China Field Army was based. They joined with Su Yu and Tan Zhenlin to hold the meeting of the General Front Committee.

In January 1949, Deng Xiaoping and Zhang Jichun jointly signed the preliminary summary report to the Central Military Commission on the operation of annihilating Huang Wei's corps, in which they summarized in detail the whole process of this operation and the experience and lessons they learned from it.

On January 6, 1949, Deng Xiaoping ordered the main forces of the East China Field Army to launch an all-out offensive against the Group led by Du Yiming, who refused to surrender. At the same time, Deng demanded that the Central Plains Field Army closely co-ordinate with the East China Field Army and prepare at any time to intercept the fleeing enemy troops and check the enemy reinforcements. The fierce battle lasted until the afternoon of January 10; during that period, over 100,000 enemy soldiers from the remnants of Du Yiming were wiped out. As of that day, the Huai-Hai Campaign, which lasted 65 days, ended victoriously. About 560,000 enemy soldiers, including the Commander Post of Kuomintang Xuzhou General Headquarters of "Suppressing Bandits," five corps headquarters, 22 army headquarters, and 56 divisions were annihilated. The broad areas on the north, to the middle and lower reaches of Changjiang River (the Yangtze River) were liberated, which exposed the central cities, such as Nanjing, Shanghai, and Wuhan, ruled by Kuomintang reactionaries, to the direct deterrence of the People's Liberation Army.

2. During the Huai-Hai Campaign, Su Yu (third from left), the Deputy-Commander of the East China Field Army, Chen Shiqu (fifth from left), the Chief of Staff, and Zhang Zhen (fourth from left), the Deputy Chief of Staff listened to the reports on the situation of the frontline of Huai-Hai.

3. The members of the General Front Committee at the Huai-Hai frontline. From left: Su Yu, Deng Xiaoping, Liu Bocheng, Chen Yi, and Tan Zhenlin.

2

3

4

5

6

7

8

4. In adhering to the operational principles set by the Party Central Committee and the Central Military Commission, the East China and Central Plains Field Armies launched the Huai-Hai Campaign from November 6, 1948, to January 10, 1949. The photo shows the troops of the East China Field Army rushing to the battlefield day and night.

5. The second phase of the Huai-Hai Campaign was to besiege and annihilate Huang Wei's Corps of Kuomintang. The photo shows that a small detachment of our army launched an attack along the Wuohe River.

6. On November 9, 1948, led by General He Jifeng and General Zhang Kexia, three and half divisions from the 57th Army and the 77th Army subordinated to Kuomintang Third Pacifying Zone rose in revolt at the front and crossed over. This revolt played a certain role in accelerating the victory of the Huai-Hai Campaign. The photo shows that the revolting troops were bound for the liberated areas.

7. On December 1, 1948, our army liberated Xuzhou City. The photo shows our army passing through Xuzhou City to pursue and wipe out the fleeing enemy troops.

8. During the Huai-Hai Campaign, the broad masses of people actively supported the front by helping our army transport ammunitions, materials, and wounded soldiers. The photo shows the people in the Central Plains shipping ammunitions to the front by handcart.

9. In March 1949, Deng Xiaoping was making a speech at the Second Plenary Session of the Seventh Party Central Committee.

10. During the period of the Second Plenary Session of the Party Seventh Central Committee, Deng Xiaoping, He Long, Nie Rongzhen, and Cai Shufan (from right) were together.

11. Deng Xiaoping (second from left) is chatting with Chen Yi during the period of the Second Plenary Session of the Party Seventh Central Committee.

9

10

11

12

12. On April 15, 1949, the leading organs of the Second Field Army held a meeting of cadres at and above the level of division commander at Tongcheng, Anhui Province, at which time Deng Xiaoping described to the participants the essence of the Second Plenary Session of the Party Seventh Central Committee.

13. In 1948, Mao Zedong (fifth from left) was photographed with comrades from the Second Bureau of the Central Military Commission at Xibaipo. Zhou Enlai (first from right), Deng Xiaoping (second from right), and Chen Yi (third from right) were also present.

13

Commanding the Campaign Across the Changjiang (Yangtze) River

1. Our troops were preparing for forcing the Changjiang River.

In early 1949, in accordance with the instructions of the Central Military Commission, the General Front Committee renamed the Central Plains Field Army and the East China Field Army as the Second Field Army and the Third Field Army, respectively. Liu Bocheng became the Commander of the reorganized Second Field Army, Deng Xiaoping as its Political Commissar, Zhang Jichun as its Deputy Political Commissar, and Li Da as its Chief of Staff. The Front Committee of the Field Army was composed of Deng Xiaoping, Liu Bocheng, Zhang Jichun, Li Da, and Chen Geng, with Deng Xiaoping as its Secretary. Based on the original seven columns, the troops were expanded to the 3rd, 4th, and 5th corps with over 280,000 soldiers. Chen Yi became the Commander and concurrently the Political Commissar of the Third Field Army, Su Yu as its Deputy Commander and concurrently the Second Political Commissar, Tan Zhenlin as its First Deputy Political Commissar, Zhang Zhen as its Chief of Staff, and Tang Liang as its Director of the Political Department. It had the 7th, 8th, 9th, and 10th corps under its command with 580,000 soldiers in total.

On February 9, 1949, Deng Xiaoping presided over the meeting of the General Front Committee in Shangqiu, and specifically discussed the issues of the timing and deployment of troops for the operation across the Changjiang River, as well as issues of strengthening the political education in the army and its logistical support.

On February 11, 1949, in order to strengthen the unified leadership for the campaign across the Changjiang River, the Central Military Commission decided that the General Front Committee with Deng Xiaoping as its Secretary would "still exercise its functions and powers as before to direct the military operations and decide on military matters." Before long, the Party Central Committee appointed Deng Xiaoping, Liu Bocheng, Zhang Jichun, Chen Geng, and others as the members of the East China Bureau of the Party Central Committee, with Deng Xiaoping as its First Secretary, Rao Shushi the Second Secretary, and Chen Yi the Third Secretary.

At the end of February, 1949, Deng Xiaoping went to Xibaipo. From March 5 to 13, Deng Xiaoping, Chen Yi, Tan Zhenlin, and others attended the Second Plenary Session of the Party Seventh Central Committee.

On March 31, 1949, on the basis of the repeated discussions by the leaders of the Second and Third Field Armies, Deng Xiaoping personally drafted and formulated the outlines implemented in the Campaigns of Nanjing-Shanghai-Hangzhou. In light of the four possible actions taken by the enemy troops after our army crossed the Changjiang River, he put forward the operational framework for our army and plans of force deployment for crossing the Changjiang River.

On April 20, 1949, Mao Zedong and Zhu De issued an order to advance towards the whole country to the People's Liberation Army. Under the leadership of the General Front Committee, over a million strong army of the Second and Third Field Armies combined launched a magnificent and dynamic campaign—the campaign across the Changjiang River. On April 23, Nanjing was liberated.

On May 12, 1949, instructed by the General Front Committee, the Third Field Army launched the Shanghai Campaign and liberated Shanghai on May 27. Then, the Campaign across the Changjiang River victoriously came to an end and over 400,000 enemy soldiers were annihilated.

After the liberation of Shanghai, in accordance with the instructions from the Central Military Commission, the General Front Committee stopped its function, and the Second and the Third Field Armies would fulfill separate operational tasks. During an over half a year period, the General Front Committee, headed by Deng Xiaoping as its Secretary, had extraordinary wisdom and adopted the flexible strategy and tactics to organize and command in a meticulous way the Huai-Hai Campaign and the Campaign across the Changjiang River, thus making tremendous contributions to the victory of the War of Liberation.

In early August 1949, Deng Xiaoping left Shanghai for Beiping and delivered a report on the period from crossing the Changjiang River to occupying Shanghai at the preparatory meeting of the Political Consultative Conference. He introduced to the delegates the work of the Second and the Third Field Armies from crossing the Changjiang River to occupying Shanghai, and the work carried out after taking over Shanghai.

2

2. Liu Bocheng, the Commander of the Second Field Army, and Deng Xiaoping, the Political Commissar of the Second Field Army were discussing the issues related to the operation across the Changjiang River.

3

3. On April 23, 1949, our army liberated Nanjing, the center of the reactionary rule of Kuomintang, proclaiming the complete collapse of "Chiang's Family Dynasty." The photo shows our army occupying the presidential palace of Kuomintang.

4. On May 27, 1949, our army liberated Shanghai. In the summer of the same year, Deng Xiaoping (second from right) and his wife Zhuo Lin (standing) were photographed with Chen Yi (fourth from left) and his wife Zhang Qian (second from left), and children from both families.

4

Leading Troops to Liberate the Greater Southwest of China

1. Deng Xiaoping at the early period of the founding of the People's Republic of China.

In July 1949, in order to liberate the southwest of China and strengthen the leadership of the southwest region, the Party Central Committee decided to set up the Southwest Bureau of the Party Central Committee and appointed Deng Xiaoping as its First Secretary, with Liu Bocheng and He Long as its Second and Third Secretaries, respectively.

In October 1949, after attending the ceremony of the founding of the People's Republic of China in Beiping, Liu Bocheng and Deng Xiaoping arrived in Xuzhou on October 22 and commanded the leading organs of the Second Field Army to advance towards the west, which reached Zhengzhou on October 23.

On November 1, 1949, Liu Bocheng and Deng Xiaoping directed the 3rd and 5th Corps of the Second Field Army and a part of the Fourth Field Army to launch the Sichuan-Guizhou Campaign. As of December 10, they liberated Guiyang, Zunyi, Chongqing, and other places one after another.

On December 2, 1949, Deng Xiaoping took the post of the Vice-Chairman of Military and Administrative Commission of Southwest China.

On December 11, 1949, He Long and Li Jingquan commanded the 18th Corps of the First Field Army to enter Sichuan Province from Shaanxi Province so as to support the powerful army led by Liu Bocheng and Deng Xiaoping in their operation to liberate the southwest of China. On December 30, the forces led by He Long entered Chengdu. Till then, the army led by Liu Bocheng and Deng Xiaoping and a part of the troops from the First and Fourth Field Armies had won brilliant achievements on the battlefield in advancing towards the southwest of China. They wiped out Kuomintang's 10 corps headquarters, 49 army headquarters, and 113 divisions, with over 900,000 soldiers in total.

In January 1950, Deng Xiaoping presided over several meetings of the members of the Standing Committee of the Southwest Bureau of the Party Central Committee to discuss certain issues of the army's advance towards Tibet. The decision was made that the 18th Army of the 5th Corps should undertake the task of advancing towards Tibet, and the Tibet Working Committee of the Party Central Committee was set up with Zhang Guohua, the Commander of the 18th Army as its Secretary, and Tan Guansan, the Political Commissar of the 18th Army as its Deputy Secretary.

In February 1950, Deng Xiaoping became the Political Commissar of the Southwest Military Region.

In March 1950, Deng Xiaoping, Liu Bocheng, and He Long jointly issued an order to suppress the bandits. By the end of 1953, the bandits in Sichuan, Guizhou, Yunnan, and Kangding were basically eliminated, and about 900,000 bandits were annihilated.

In August 1950, Deng Xiaoping and others issued an order to launch the Changdu Campaign. The troops on their way to Tibet were instructed, on October 6, to launch an offensive; they forced the Jinsha River and liberated Changdu on October 24. They defeated over 5,700 reactionary Tibetan soldiers, which catalyzed the revolt of one Tibetan Daiben (Daiben means a unit of about 500 soldiers in the organizational structure of the Tibetan army) and surrender of four more Daiben and the office of Changdu General Administration. The victory of the Changdu Campaign opened the door to Tibet and laid a foundation for the peaceful liberation of Tibet. On May 23, 1951, Agreement by the Central People's Government and Tibetan Local Government on the Methods of Peaceful Liberation of Tibet was signed in Beijing, and it proclaimed the peaceful liberation of Tibet.

2

3

4

2. Deng Xiaoping (left) and Liu Bocheng were discussing issues concerning the deployment of the army advancing towards the southwest of China.

3. In October 1949, after attending the ceremony of the founding of the People's Republic of China, Deng Xiaoping embarked on the journey towards the southwest of China. Deng Xiaoping (second from left) was photographed with Chen Yi (third from left), Liu Bocheng (fifth from left), and Su Yu (sixth from left) at a railway station of Xuzhou City.

4. Deng Xiaoping, on his way to southwest China by train, passed through Zhengzhou.

5

5. In October 1949, Liu Bocheng and Deng Xiaoping commanded the troops to advance from Wuhan via Changsha towards southern China. The photo shows the army preparing to cross the river at Tieshan Ferry Crossing (Deng Xiaoping, center, in leather jacket).

6. On November 30, 1949, the army led by Liu Bocheng and Deng Xiaoping liberated Chongqing. On December 30, He Long directed his troops to enter Chengdu. On February 4, 1950, Deng Xiaoping joined with He Long in Chongqing. From right: Deng Xiaoping, Chen Xilian, Liu Bocheng, He Long, and Wang Weizhou.

7. Liu Bocheng (right), the Commander of the Second Field Army, together with Deng Xiaoping, the Political Commissar of the Second Field Army.

6

7

8. Deng Xiaoping (first from left), Liu Bocheng, and others discussing the issues pertinent to the liberation of southwestern China.

9. A group photo of the vice-chairmen of the Military and Administrative Commission of Southwest China. From right: Deng Xiaoping, He Long, Xiong Kewu, Long Yun, Wang Weizhou, and Liu Wenhui.

8

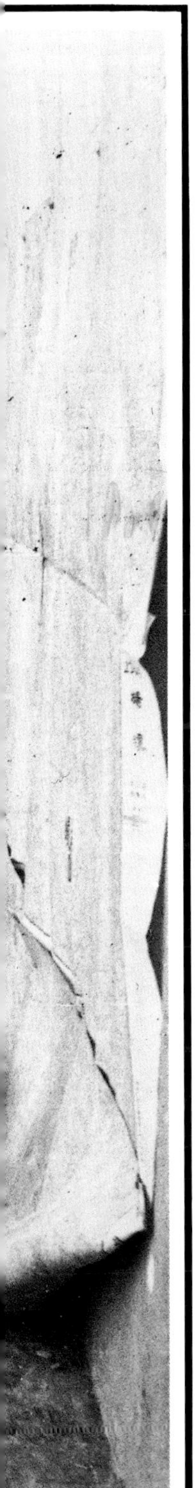

9

10

11

12

10. In July 1950, Deng Xiaoping made a speech at the First Plenary Session of the Military and Administrative Commission of Southwest China.

11. In 1950, Deng Xiaoping made a speech at a gathering of combat heroes and exemplary fighters.

12. From April to August 1950, the engineering corps built a 600-kilometer-long highway from Ya'an to Ganzhi in order to guarantee the material supply to the troops on their way to Tibet. The photo shows a grand mobilization rally attended by the engineering corps who would construct the highway.

13

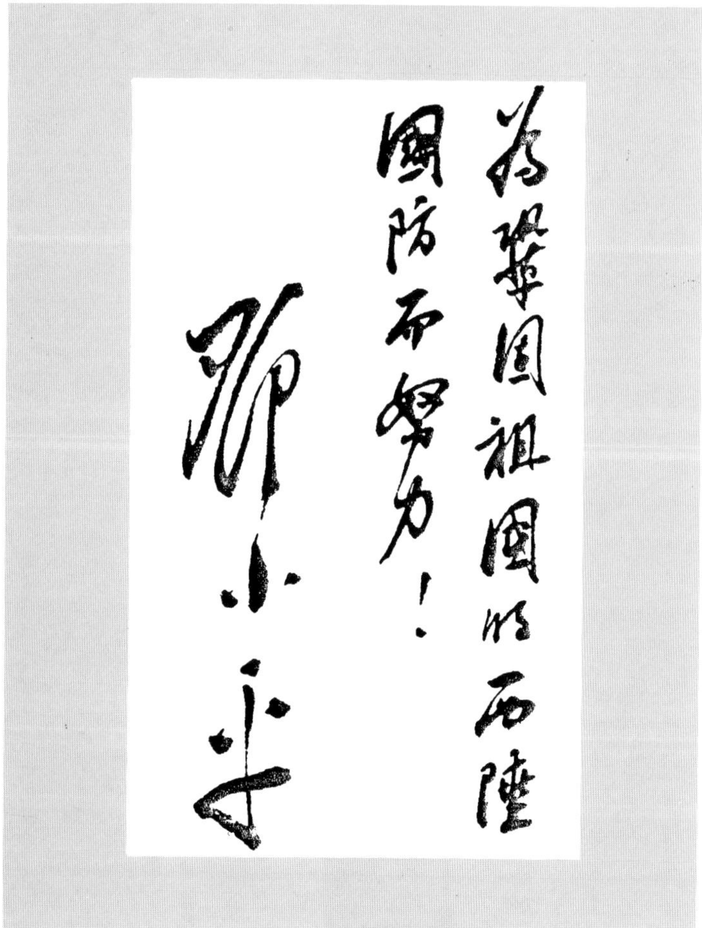

14

13. On October 6, 1950, our army launched the Changdu Campaign and took Changdu at one blow. The photo shows that our army officers were explaining the Party's policies toward the ethnic nationalities to the revolted officers and men of the 9th Daiben of Tibetan army.

14. The calligraphy by Deng Xiaoping: "Make efforts to consolidate the national defense on the west border area!"

15. In April 1951, when the delegation of the Tibetan Local Government headed by Ngatoi Ngawang Jigme (left) passed Chongqing on its way to Beijing for negotiation, it received a warm welcome by Deng Xiaoping (right) and other military and administrative leaders, as well as masses of the southwest region.

16. On October 26, 1951, our army entered and stationed in Lhasa, Tibet. The photo shows people from all circles in Lhasa held a mass rally to welcome the Liberation Army.

15

16

17

17. In 1952, Deng Xiaoping (fifth from left, front row) and He Long (fourth from left, front row) were photographed with the high-ranking cadres of the Southwest Military Region.

18. Deng Xiaoping personally led the "movement against three evils" (The movement against three evils, i.e. corruption, waste, and bureaucracy, launched within the Party and government organs from the end of 1951 to the fall of 1952) in the Southwest Military Region. The photo shows Deng Xiaoping reading and commenting on certain documents.

18

19

19. In 1952, Deng Xiaoping and He Long were at the First Sport Games of the Southwest Region.

Showing Concern for New China's National Defense and the Building of the Army

1. Deng Xiaoping was an important member in the leading collective of the first generation of our Party, just as comrade Mao Zedong was the core.

In July 1952, Deng Xiaoping was transferred from the Southwest Bureau of the Party Central Committee and the Southwest Military Region to work in the Party Central Committee and the Central Government.

In September 1954, Deng Xiaoping was elected to be the Vice-Chairman of the National Defense Council at the First Session of the First National People's Congress. In the same month, he was also appointed as a member of the Military Commission of the Party Central Committee.

In November 1955, Deng Xiaoping, Liu Shaoqi, He Long, and other leaders from the Party, government, and army went to Dalian to watch the military exercises of anti-amphibious operation and inspect troops there.

At the Chengdu Meeting held in March 1958, the Party Central Committee discussed and adopted the views on the work of national defense prepared by Deng Xiaoping.

On August 1, 1958, Deng Xiaoping, Liu Shaoqi, Zhu De, and others visited the Exhibition on Scientific and Technological Achievements in the National Defense and were photographed with the working staff there.

In August 1958, Deng Xiaoping summoned Zhang Guohua, Deng Shaodong, and others to Beijing, and he clearly elaborated on the policies and strategies set by the Party Central Committee on putting down a rebellion launched by the reactionary clique of Tibetan upper-class and gave them some important directives.

In January 1960, Deng Xiaoping attended the enlarged meeting of the Central Military Commission held in Guangzhou to study and deliberate the issues regarding strategic principles and the building of the national defense.

On March 26, 1960, Deng Xiaoping, Zhou Enlai, and Zhu De received the delegates attending the Conference of the Political Work of the Whole Army.

On April 23, 1960, Deng Xiaoping, along with Mao Zedong and Zhu De, received all delegates attending the National Conference of the People's Militia.

On May 17, 1960, Deng Xiaoping and others received the delegates participating in the First Working Conference of the Staff Officer from the Armored Force and the delegates participating in the other two conferences. In the same month, he joined others in receiving the delegates attending the Conference of Activists in Cultural and Educational Fields of the People's Liberation Army and delegates from four other meetings.

At the end of February 1963, Deng Xiaoping, together with Mao Zedong, Liu Shaoqi, Zhou Enlai, Zhu De, and others received the delegates attending the Conference of the Political Work of the Whole Army and the Conference of the Political Work of the Air Force.

In January 1964, Deng Xiaoping, together with Mao Zedong, Liu Shaoqi, and others received all the delegates attending the Conference of the Political Work of the Whole Army and other conferences. In the same month, he delivered a report on the current international and domestic situation at the Conference of the Political Work of the Whole Army.

In mid-June 1964, Deng Xiaoping, along with Mao Zedong, Liu Shaoqi, Zhou Enlai, Zhu De, and others watched the demonstration of achievement in military training by the troops from Beijing Military Region and Jinan Military Region. They highly praised and commended the demo troops and the people's militia.

In January 1965, Deng Xiaoping attended the plenary session of the National Defense Council to discuss the building of the national defense. In the same month, he, along with Mao Zedong, Liu Shaoqi, Zhou Enlai, and others received the delegates participating in the Whole Army's Conference on Logistic Works.

On May 19, 1965, Deng Xiaoping, together with Liu Shaoqi, Zhou Enlai, Zhu De, and others received all the delegates attending the Conference for Military Operation of the Central Military Commission. On the same day, he participated in receiving the graduates of the 12th enrollment of the Logistic Academy of the Liberation Army.

In May 1965, Deng Xiaoping, Zhou Enlia, and other leaders from central government received the whole staff who had participated in the first and second nuclear tests.

On August 17, 1965, Deng Xiaoping, together with Mao Zedong, Liu Shaoqi, Zhou Enlai, and others received the representatives from meritorious army units who joined the "August 6" sea battle.

Soon after the start of the "Great Cultural Revolution," Deng Xiaoping was erroneously repudiated and subjected to political persecution. He was deprived of all leading posts in the Party, government, and army.

After the "Lin Biao Event" occurred in 1971, Deng Xiaoping wrote a letter from Jiangxi Province to the Party Central Committee, in which he expressed his firm support to the resolution adopted by the Party Central Committee on the Lin Biao anti-Party clique.

2

3

2. In 1952, He Long, Deng Xiaoping, Nie Rongzhen, and Luo Ruiqin (from right) at the First Sport Games of the Whole Army.

3. In October 1949, Deng Xiaoping was appointed as a member of the Chinese People's Revolutionary Military Commission. A group photo of some members of the Commission was taken in front of Yinian Hall in Zhongnanhai in 1952 (Deng Xiaoping, third from right, second row).

4

5

4. Deng Xiaoping watching the chess game between Zhu De and Peng Dehuai.

5. In 1955, the Party and State leaders were photographed with the deputies from the Liberation Army attending the Second Plenary Session of the First National People's Congress. From right: Deng Xiaoping, Peng Dehuai, Chen Yun, Zhou Enlai, Zhu De, Mao Zedong, Liu Shaoqi, and Soong Ching Ling.

6

6. On October 18, 1954, a group photo was taken of the whole members of the First Session of the National Defense Council of the People's Republic of China. From left, front row: Long Yun, Zhang Zhizhong, Ye Jianying, Xu Xiangqian, Deng Xiaoping, Liu Bocheng, Zhu De, Mao Zedong, Peng Dehuai, He Long, Luo Ronghuan, Nie Rongzhen, Cheng Qian, and Fu Zuoyi.

7

7. In 1955, Deng Xiaoping (third from left), Chen Yi (first from left), He Long (second from left), and Huang Kecheng (fourth from left) sitting on the viewing stand to watch the shooting sport games of the whole army.

8

9

8. In 1955, Deng Xiaoping (second from left at third row), Liu Shaoqi (left at first row), and Ye Jianying (right at first row) watching the military exercises of anti-amphibious operation in Luda.

9. Deng Xiaoping (left) and Nie Rongzhen at the viewing stand for the military exercise.

10. Deng Xiaoping (first from right, front), Nie Rongzhen (first from left), and Luo Ronghuan (second from left) visiting the Exhibition on the Air Defense Force Equipment.

11. On August 1, 1958, Liu Shaoqi, Zhu De, Deng Xiaoping, and others were photographed with the working staff for the Exhibition on the Scientific and Technological Achievements in the National Defense. From left at front row: Lin Boqu, Zhu De, Liu Shaoqi, Deng Xiaoping, Peng Dehuai, and Ye Jianying.

12. Deng Xiaoping (left) having a cordial conversation with Peng Dehuai while visiting the Exhibition on the Scientific and Technological Achievements in the National Defense.

10

11

12

13

13. Deng Xiaoping (left) and He Long walking into the Great Hall of the People.

14. In May 1959, Deng Xiaoping (second from left), Liu Shaoqi, and other Party and State leaders received the delegates attending the Conference of Exemplary Working Units and Activists of the Logistic Departments of the Whole Army.

15. In August 1959, Deng Xiaoping (seventh from left, front row), Liu Shaoqi, and others were photographed with all the members attending the meeting of the National Defense Council.

14

15

16

16. Deng Xiaoping (from left at front row), Liu Shaoqi, Zhou Enlai, Li Fuchun, and others receiving the delegates attending the Conference of Activists of the Engineering Corps of the Liberation Army.

17. In 1961, Deng Xiaoping (from left), Chen Yi, He Long, Peng Zhen, and Li Fuchun watching the soccer game at Beijing Worker's Stadium.

17

18

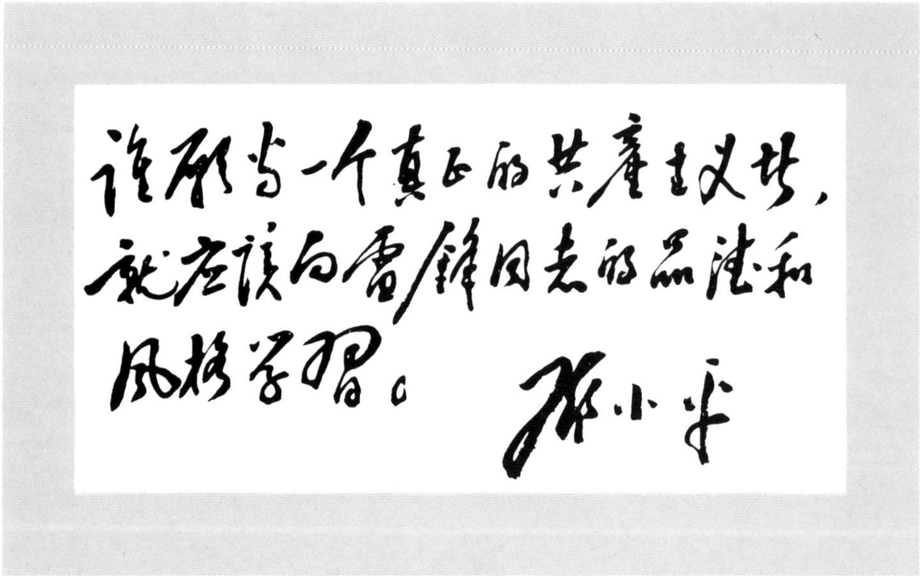
谁愿当一个真正的共产主义者，
就应该向雷锋同志的品德和
风格学习。
邓小平

19

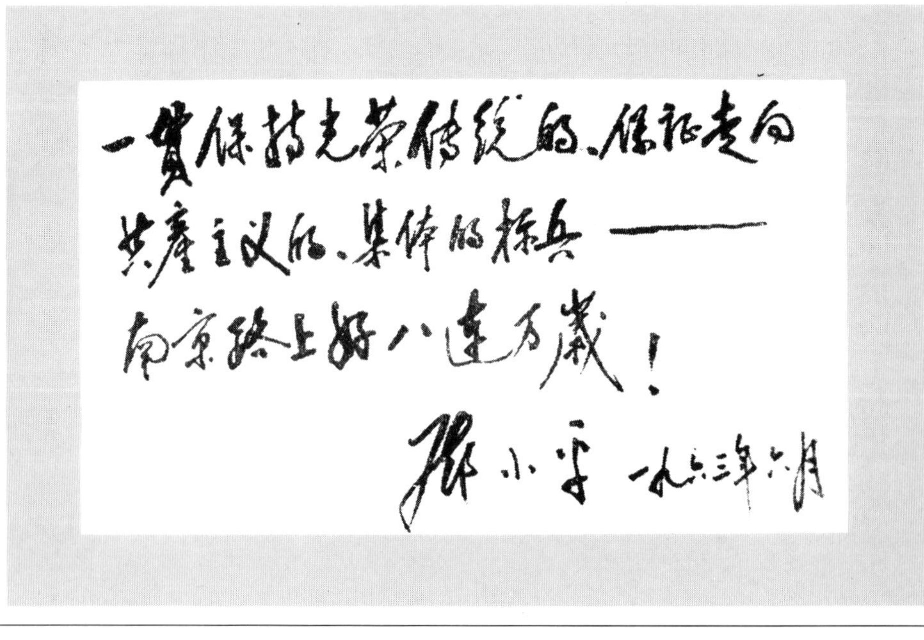
一贯保持光荣传统的、保证走向
共产主义的、集体的标兵——
南京路上好八连万岁！
邓小平 一九六三年六月

20

21

18. On November 1, 1961, Deng Xiaoping made a report on the international and domestic situation at the Conference of the Political Work of the Whole Army.

19. In March 1963, Deng Xiaoping autographed his calligraphy calling upon the people to learn from comrade Lei Feng.

20. In June 1963, Deng Xiaoping wrote a calligraphy for the "Good Eighth Company on the Nanjian Road," Shanghai.

21. Deng Xiaoping and Peng Zhen with their wives watching a basketball game between "August 1" team of the Liberation Army and the Soviet Union army team.

22. In January 1964, Deng Xiaoping delivered a report on the current situation to the delegates attending the Conference of the Political Work of the Whole Army. Xiao Hua (right), the Director of the General Political Department of the People's Liberation Army.

22

23

23. In 1964, Deng Xiaoping (right), Zhou Enlai (center), and Luo Ruiqing looking at the light machine guns used by the troops participating in the military skill competitions.

24. At the Ming Tombs reservoir near Beijing, Deng Xiaoping watching the demonstration by the engineering detachment from the Jinan Command.

25. Deng Xiaoping (center) listening to the report by Yang Chengwu, the Deputy Chief of the General Staff on military training of the troops.

26. Mao Zedong and other Party and State leaders were photographed with the officers and soldiers from the troops participating in the demonstration of military training. From left at front row: Dong Biwu, Deng Xiaoping, Zhu De, Mao Zedong, Liu Shaoqi, Zhou Enlai, and He Long.

24

25

26

27

28

27. In January 1965, Deng Xiaoping attended the meeting of the National Defense Council presided over by Chairman Liu Shaoqi. From left on the rostrum: Fu Zuoyi, Cheng Qian, Ye Jianying, Chen Yi, Liu Shaoqi, He Long, Deng Xiaoping, Luo Ruiqing, Zhang Zhizhong, and Cai Tingkai.

28. In 1965, Deng Xiaoping (second from right, front) and Li Fuchun (third from right, front) inspected the ordnance factory.

29. In November 1965, Deng Xiaoping (first from left, front), accompanied by Li Jingquan (first from right) and Cheng Zihua (second from right) personally went to inspect the construction site of the "Third Line" projects (refers to projects in the remote regions away from the coastal areas).

29

30 31

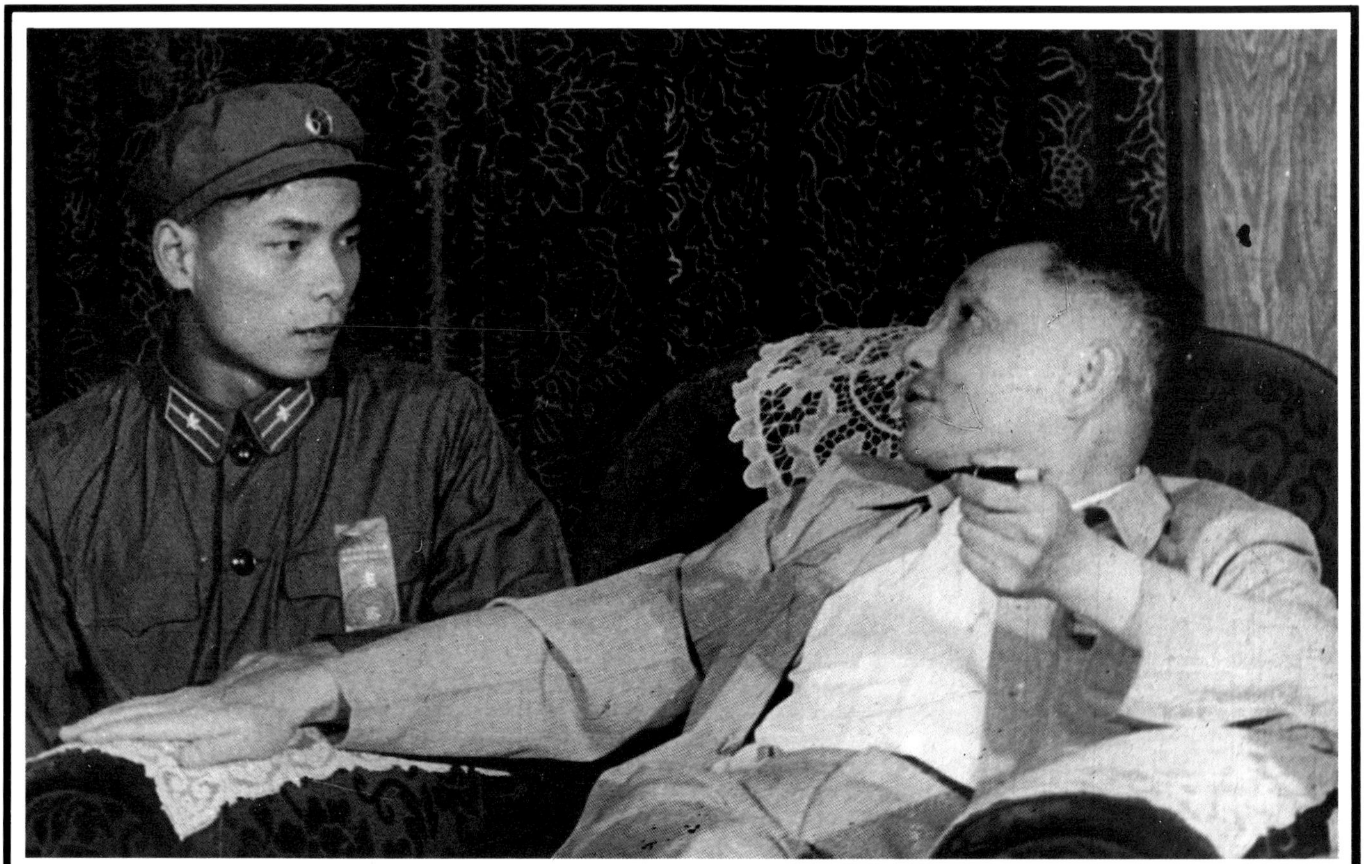

30. In May 1965, Deng Xiaoping (sixth from the front row), Zhou Enlai (eighth from left), and other central Party leading members received the staff participating in the first and second nuclear tests and were photographed with them.

31. In May 1965, during the intermission of the Ninth National Congress of the Communist Youth League of China, Deng Xiaoping having a talk with the delegates from the Liberation Army.

32. In January 1966, Deng Xiaoping, Liu Shaoqi, Zhou Enlai, Song Qingling (Soong Ching Ling), and others attended the grand party held in the Capital, Beijing, with the theme "Army supports the government and loves the people, while government supports the army and gives preferential treatment to the families of the armymen and survivors of the martyrs."

32

33

33. In 1966, during the early period of the "Great Cultural Revolution," Deng Xiaoping (left), Liu Shaoqi (center), and Zhou Enlai at the rostrum of Tian An Men.

Becoming the Chief of the General Staff of the People's Liberation Army

1. Deng Xiaoping in 1975.

On December 12, 1973, at the meeting of the Political Bureau of the Party Central Committee, Mao Zedong recommended Deng Xiaoping as a member of the Political Bureau and the Chief of the General Staff of the People's Liberation Army. On December 22, Deng Xiaoping became a member of the Central Military Commission and participated in its leadership.

In January 1974, Deng Xiaoping became one of a five-member leading group (including Ye Jianying and Chen Xilian) of the Central Military Commission in charge of daily work and emergency matters of preparing against war. In the same month, he took a leading part in cross-region transfer of the commanders of the eight military regions, and his work was highly appraised by Mao Zedong.

On the recommendation of Mao Zedong, the Party Central Committee issued No. 1 document on January 25, 1975, and appointed Deng Xiaoping as the Vice-Chairman of the Central Military Commission and concurrently the Chief of General Staff of the People's Liberation Army.

On January 25, 1975, Deng Xiaoping made an important speech on the consolidation of the army at the meeting of cadres at and above the level of regimental commander from the offices of the Headquarters of the General Staff of the Liberation Army. He stressed that the total number of the army should be reduced, those excessive not-on-staff-table cadres should be reassigned, the fine tradition should be restored, and various kinds of policies should be implemented. He pointed out: "In the movement of rectification of the army, the first thing to do is to enhance the sense of being a Party member and eliminate factionalism, and the second is to strengthen the discipline."

In the first half of the year 1975, Deng Xiaoping waged a tit-for-tat struggle against Jiang Qing and her followers for their feverishly carrying out the movement to oppose the so-called "empiricism." According to the views of Mao Zedong, Deng Xiaoping chaired the meetings several times of the Political Bureau of the Party Central Committee, and seriously criticized Jiang Qing for her wrongdoings regarding factional activities and so-called "anti-empiricism movement."

On July 15, 1975, Deng Xiaoping delivered a speech on the tasks for army consolidation at the enlarged meeting of the Central Military Commission, pointing out unequivocally that the tasks for army consolidation were to eliminate the problems of swelling, loitering, arrogance, extravagance, and sluggishness.

On August 3, 1975, Deng Xiaoping made a speech on the consolidation of the industrial enterprises of national defense at the meeting of major enterprises in national defense industry.

From October 1975 to March 1976, Deng Xiaoping was wrongly criticized in the movement of "Repudiating Deng Xiaoping and Counterattacking the Wind of Reversing the Verdicts by Right-deviationist." After the "Tian An Men Incident" in April 1976, he was deprived of all his posts both inside and outside the Party, with the exception of his party membership.

In July 1977, the Third Plenary Session of the Tenth Central Committee of the Chinese Communist Party decided to reinstate Deng Xiaoping in his former posts of the Party, government, and the army. After he came back to work, he brought order out of chaos, sought truth from facts, opposed the views of two "any-and-alls" (refers to a wording in the joint editorial entitled "Study Documents Well and Grasp the Key Link" of the *People's Daily*, the *Red Flag* magazine, and the *Liberation Army Daily* published on February 7, 1977, in which it maintained that "we will resolutely uphold any and all policy decisions made by Chairman Mao; we will unswervingly adhere to any and all of Chairman Mao's directives").

On August 23, 1977, in addressing the symposium organized by the Central Military Commission, Deng Xiaoping reiterated that the education and training of the army should be placed high on the strategic position. In this connection, he demanded the strengthening of the training of the army and the improvement of the management of various military academies.

On December 28, 1977, in his address to the plenary meeting of the Central Military Commission, Deng Xiaoping focused on the criticizing of the "Gang of Four" and on the following five points: (1) consolidating the leading bodies at all levels; (2) the international and domestic situation; (3) managing the army like managing a large school; (4) improving the discipline; and (5) strengthening the unity.

On May 13, 1978, in a conversation with the leaders of the General Staff Headquarters, Deng Xiaoping pointed out that the commanding system should be gradually modernized.

On June 2, 1978, in a speech made at the Conference of the Political Work of the Whole Army, Deng Xiaoping talked about the following four issues: new historical conditions; seeking truth from facts; doing away with the old ideas and establishing the new ones; and doing things by setting an example for others. He stressed that seeking truth from facts was the starting point and fundamental principle of Mao Zedong Thought.

On July 11, 1978, in listening to the progress reports for the preparation of the Working Meeting of the National People's Militia, Deng Xiaoping pointed out that great attention should be paid to the work of people's militia under the modern conditions.

On July 29, 1979, in meeting with the participants of the enlarged meeting of the Standing Committee of the Party Committee of the Navy, Deng Xiaoping made a speech on implementation of the ideological line and political line guaranteed by the organizational line. He stressed the importance of the serious selection and training of successors, and put forward that the building of the navy should be focused on real combat effectiveness.

On March 2, 1980, Deng Xiaoping resigned from his posts of the Chief of General Staff and the First Secretary of the Party Committee of the General Staff Headquarters. In December of the same year, he delivered a speech on streamlining the army and enhancing the combat effectiveness at the enlarged meeting of the Standing Committee of the Central Military Commission. He especially emphasized the importance of eliminating the phenomenon of swelling, the reform of the structure and training, as well as the improvement of the political and ideological work.

In October 1980, on Deng Xiaoping's suggestion, the Central Military Commission held a seminar in Beijing attended by the high-ranking cadres from the whole army. Its key topic was what kind of strategy would be adopted in the future anti-aggression wars. On October 15, in his conclusive speech on this topic, Deng Xiaping pointed out that he, "preferred the strategy of active defense in the future anti-aggression wars. The active defense is not merely defense, which embodies the attack. The active defense itself also contains the meaning of protracted operations. We have always based ourselves on the principle of overcoming the strong by the weak, using inferior equipment to fight against enemies with modern equipment and carrying on the protracted war to exhaust the enemy's strength. Therefore, our strategic principle is that of the active defense."

2. On May 1, 1973 (the International Labor Day), Deng Xiaoping (second from right) watched a performance by the art troupe of Beijing Military Region at Summer Palace in Beijing.

3. In 1973, Deng Xiaoping (left at front) and Xu Xiangqian at the Capital Airport.

2

3

4

4. When he was in charge of the daily work of the Party Central Committee in 1975, Deng Xiaoping chaired a series of important meetings to solve the problems concerning the army and other fields. He boldly and resolutely took measures to consolidate the army, which were welcomed by all officers and men.

5. In July 1977, Deng Xiaoping at the Third Plenary Session of the Party Tenth Central Committee.

6. In 1977, Deng Xiaoping (from right at front), Ye Jianying, Xu Shiyou, and others in Guangzhou.

5

6

7

8

7. On August 22, 1977, Deng Xiaoping (first from right) and Ye Jianying meeting with the delegates attending the Eleventh National Congress of the Chinese Communist Party.

8. On December 14, 1977, Deng Xiaoping (right) was together with Xu Xiangqian.

9. In 1977, Deng Xiaoping shook hands with performers from the army troops in Guangzhou.

9

10

11

10. On January 14, 1977, Deng Xiaoping (left) and his wife Zhuo Lin went to visit Ye Jianying at his home.

11. On August 23, 1977, Deng Xiaoping (center) made an important speech at the symposium held by the Central Military Commission. Nie Rongzhen (left) and Xu Xiangqian (right) were at the symposium.

12. On December 12, 1977, Deng Xiaoping was present at the enlarged meeting of the Central Military Commission.

13. On August 1, 1977, Deng Xiaoping attended the reception to celebrate the 50th anniversary of the founding of the People's Liberation Army.

12

13

14

15

14. **On March 15, 1978, the 20th anniversary of the establishment of the Military Science Academy, Deng Xiaoping (left) and Ye Jianying received the whole staff of that academy.**

15. **Deng Xiaoping (right) shaking hands with Song Shilun, the President of the Military Science Academy.**

16. **On March 15, 1978, Deng Xiaoping wrote the following calligraphy for the Military Science Academy, "Follow Mao Zedong's military thought, research into people's war under modern conditions, and develop military science of our army."**

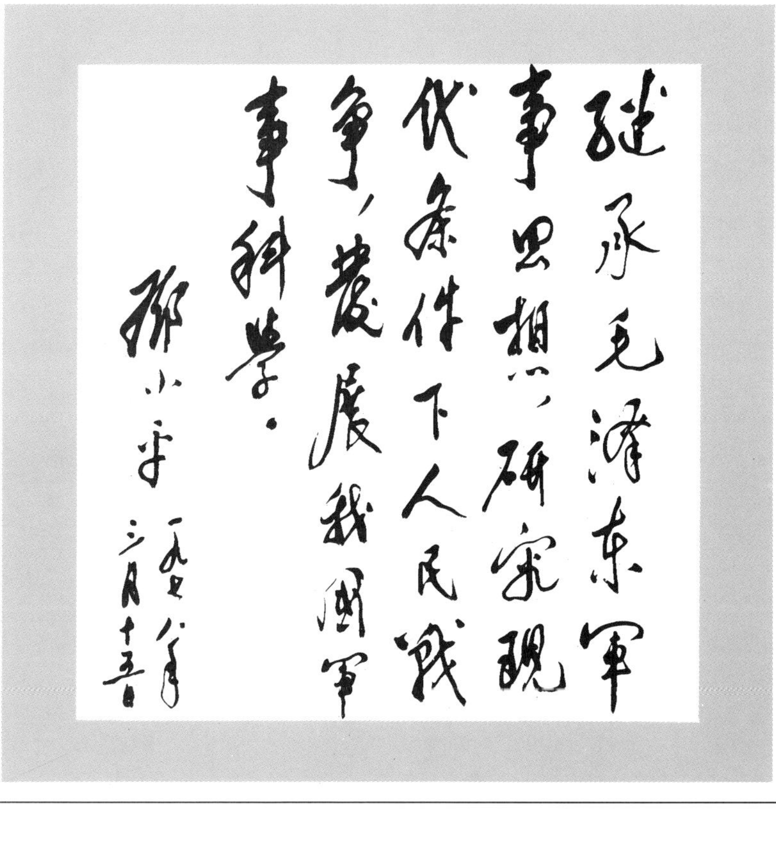

16

17

17. In March 1978, Deng Xiaoping (first from right) came to visit the deputies from the army to attend the Fifth National People's Congress.

18. In May 1978, Deng Xiaoping (right at front) and Ye Jianying, who was responsible for the work of the Central Military Commission, were at the Conference of the Political Work of the Whole Army.

19. In September 1978, accompanied by Li Desheng, the Commander of the Shenyang Military Region, and others, Deng Xiaoping (second from right) was visiting the factory.

18

19

20

22

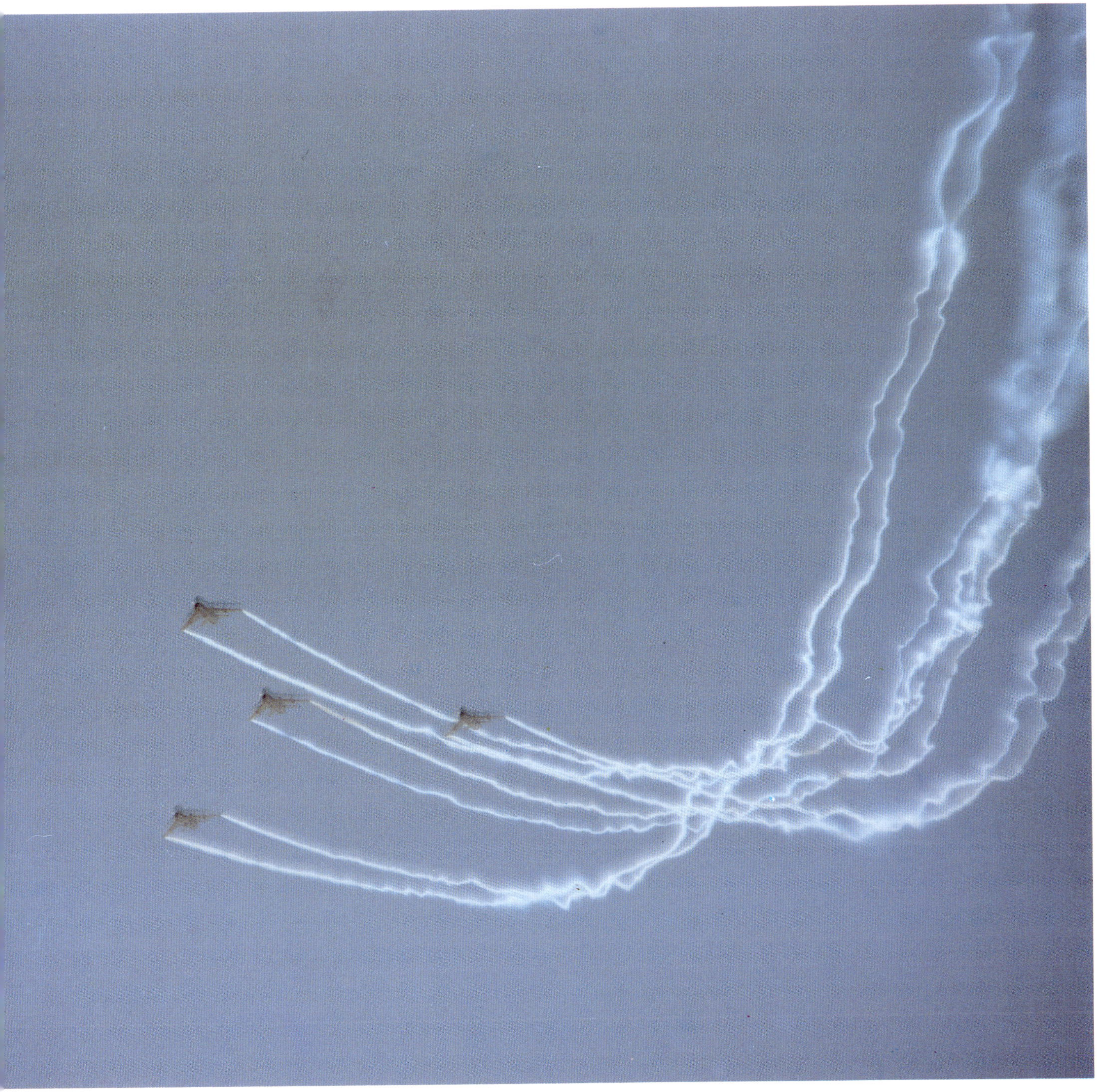

21

20-21. Deng Xiaoping watching the air show of aerobatic flight.

22. On October 12, 1978, while watching the air show of aerobatic flight by the air force, Deng Xiaoping listening to the reports by Zhang Tingfa, the Commander of the Air Force.

23

23. After watching the air show of aerobatic flight by the air force, Deng Xiaoping (right) and Ye Jianying shook hands with pilots.

24. In October 1978, Deng Xiaoping (first from left) and Ye Jianying were receiving pilots who participated in the demonstration of military training at Yangcun Airport.

25. On May 31, 1979, Deng Xiaoping was photographed with members of Heroes and Exemplary Fighters Reporting Group from the war of self-defensive counterattack on the Sino-Vietnam border region. From left at front: Deng Xiaoping, Wang Zhen, and Ulan Fu.

24

25

26

27

28

26. On July 29, 1979, Deng Xiaoping (center) made an important speech about the criterion of truth at the enlarged meeting of the Party Committee of the Navy.

27. Deng Xiaoping (first from right), while inspecting the North Sea Fleet, was listening to reports by the leaders of the Navy.

28. On August 2, 1979, Deng Xiaoping was together with officers and men of the naval warship while inspecting the North Sea Fleet.

29

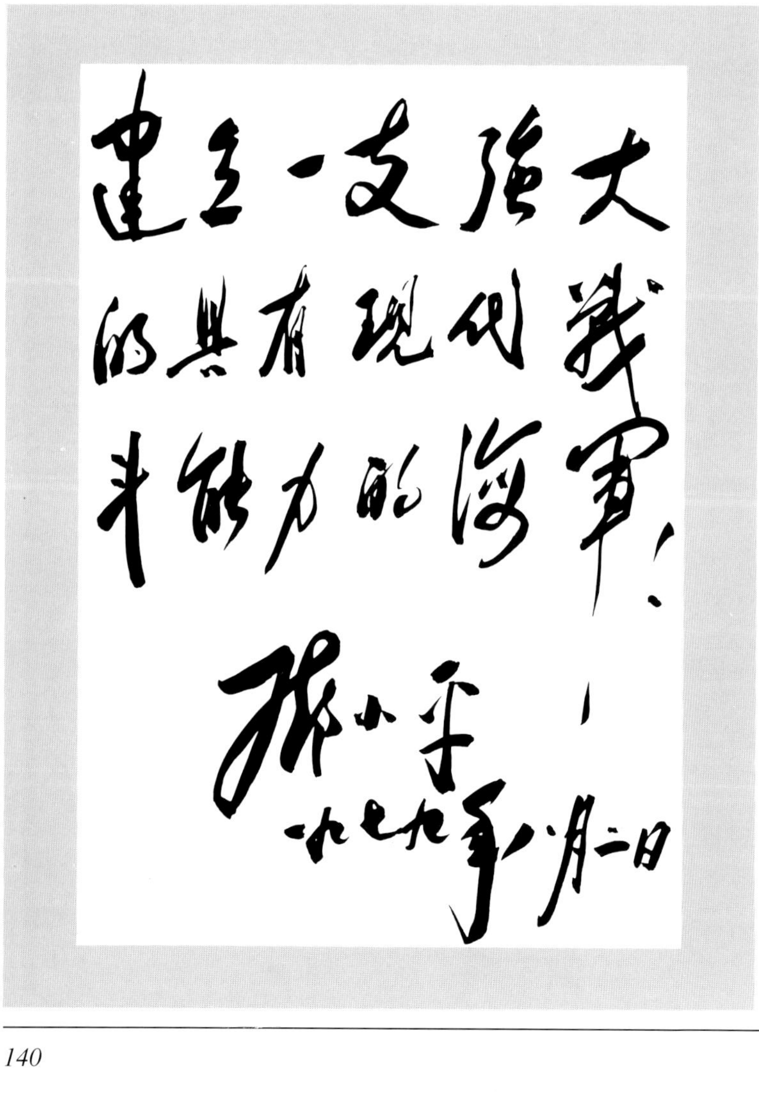

30

31

29. On August 2, 1979, Deng Xiaoping wrote a calligraphy for No. 105 warship of the navy.

30. Deng Xiaoping's calligraphy.

31. In 1979, Deng Xiaoping made an important speech at the enlarged meeting of the Central Military Commission. From left: Chen Xilian, Yang Yong, Yang Dezhi, Wei Guoqing, Yang Shangkun, Deng Xiaoping, Geng Biao, and Zhang Tingfa.

32. On July 10, 1980, Deng Xiaoping chatting with Xu Shiyou (right) during intervals of the Third Session of the Fifth National People's Congress.

32

33

33. On May 18, 1980, Deng Xiaoping (right), Nie Rongzhen (center), Wang Zhen, and others went to the Command Post of the Commission of Science, Technology, and Industry for National Defense to watch the launching experiment of the first intercontinental missile made in China.

The Commander of the Three Armed Services

1. Deng Xiaoping, Chairman of the Central Military Commission.

In June 1981, Deng Xiaoping was elected to be Chairman of the Central Military Commission at the Sixth Plenary Session of the Party Eleventh Central Committee.

On September 13, 1981, a real-life military exercise of the front army, the largest ever since the founding of the People's Republic of China, was formally held somewhere in North China. Deng Xiaoping gave many important directives to this grand military exercise, and personally went to the field to watch it with other leaders from the Party, government, and army. On September 19, Deng Xiaoping reviewed the troops participating in the exercise and made a speech on building a powerful, modernized, and regularized revolutionary army.

On July 4, 1982, in his address to the symposium held by the Central Military Commission, Deng Xiaoping emphasized that institutional reform should be backed by adequate rules and regulations, sound working methods, and appropriate leadership approaches. He also pointed out that institutional reform in the army should contribute to the selection and promotion of qualified personnel and the improvement of efficiency.

On December 28, 1982, the meeting of chiefs of staff from the whole army was held in Beijing. Deng Xiaoping gave important instructions on strengthening the building of army and received all meeting participants, together with other leaders of the Party Central Committee and the Central Military Commission.

On October 1, 1984, a grand review of troops and mass parade were held to celebrate the 35th anniversary of the founding of the People's Republic of China. Deng Xiaoping reviewed the troops and delivered an important speech.

On November 1, 1984, at the symposium held by the Central Military Commission, Deng Xiaoping said that the army should put the interest of the national construction above everything else.

On June 4, 1985, Deng Xiaoping addressed the enlarged meeting of the Central Military Commission, announcing the reduction of the People's Liberation Army's military strength by one million. He further pointed out that the current disarmament demonstrated the strength and confidence of the Chinese Communist Party, Chinese Government, and Chinese People.

On October 16, 1986, Deng Xiaoping presided over the memorial service for Liu Bocheng, and subsequently wrote an article entitled "Memorizing Bocheng," which was published in the *People's Daily*.

On July 31, 1987, Deng Xiaoping attended the rally to celebrate the 60th Anniversary of the Founding of the People's Liberation Army held in the Capital, Beijing, and met with deputies attending the Conference of the Heroes and Exemplary Fighters of the Whole Army. On August 1, Deng Xiaoping wrote the following calligraphy for the 60th anniversary of the founding of the People's Liberation Army: "Striving to build our army into a powerful, modernized, and regularized revolutionary army."

On November 2, 1987, Deng Xiaoping was re-elected to be Chairman of the Central Military Commission at the First Plenary Session of the Party Thirteenth Central Committee.

On September 14, 1988, Deng Xiaoping met with 17 high-ranking military officers who were granted the ranks of general and was photographed with them at Huairen Hall, Zhongnanhai.

In June 1989, at Huairen Hall, Zhongnanhai, Deng Xiaoping received cadres at and above the level of army commander from the troops enforcing martial law in the Capital. He stressed in the meeting that no matter how the older generations were replaced by the new, our army would always be under the leadership of the Party, always be the defender of the nation, socialism, and the interest of the people, and our armymen were the most beloved ones.

2. In June 1981, Deng Xiaoping was elected to be Chairman of the Central Military Commission at the Sixth Plenary Session of the Thirteenth Central Committee of the Chinese Communist Party.

3. In August 1981, accompanied by Xiao Hua, the Political Commissar of Lanzhou Military Region, and others, Deng Xiaoping (left) inspected the border regions in the northwest of China.

2

3

4

5

4. In September 1981, Deng Xiaoping, standing on the car, reviewed the troops participating in the military exercise held somewhere in North China.

5. Deng Xiaoping (left) and Hu Yaobang at the reviewing stand.

6-7. Deng Xiaoping (right) and Qin Jiwei watching the joint exercise by the infantry and tank units.

7

6

9

10

8-9. Deng Xiaoping watching the military exercise.

10. Deng Xiaoping (second from left), Chairman of the Central Military Commission, shaking hands with commanders of the troops participating in the military exercise.

11

11. The military review was held after the military exercise.

12. Deng Xiaoping (right at front), Ye Jianying, Chen Yun, Nie Rongzhen, Xu Xiangqian, and others receiving the officers and men from the troops participating in the military exercise.

12

13

14

13. On October 9, 1981, Deng Xiaoping (right) met with Li Mo'an, the former general of Kuomintang army, who came from the United States to attend the meeting to celebrate the 70th anniversary of the Revolution of 1911 (the Chinese revolution led by Dr. Sun Yat-sen which overthrew the Qing Dynasty).

14. On October 4, 1981, Deng Xiaoping (center) and Deng Yingchao (left) received Huang Zhicheng, an air force major of Kuomintang who revolted and returned from Taiwan to the mainland.

15

15. In January 1982, Deng Xiaoping receiving the participants of the Conference of the Political Work of the Whole Army.

16. In July 1982, Deng Xiaoping (first from left) delivered an important speech at the symposium held by the Central Military Commission. Geng Biao (second from left) and Zhang Tingfa (third from left) were also present.

16

17

17. In July 1982, Deng Xiaoping and Chen Yun receiving the participants of the symposium held by the Central Military Commission.

18. At Bangchui Island in August 1983, Deng Xiaoping received the leaders from the troops stationed in Luda.

19. In 1984, Deng Xiaoping (first from left) and Wang Zhen (second from left) received the leaders of the troops stationed in Xiamen.

18

19

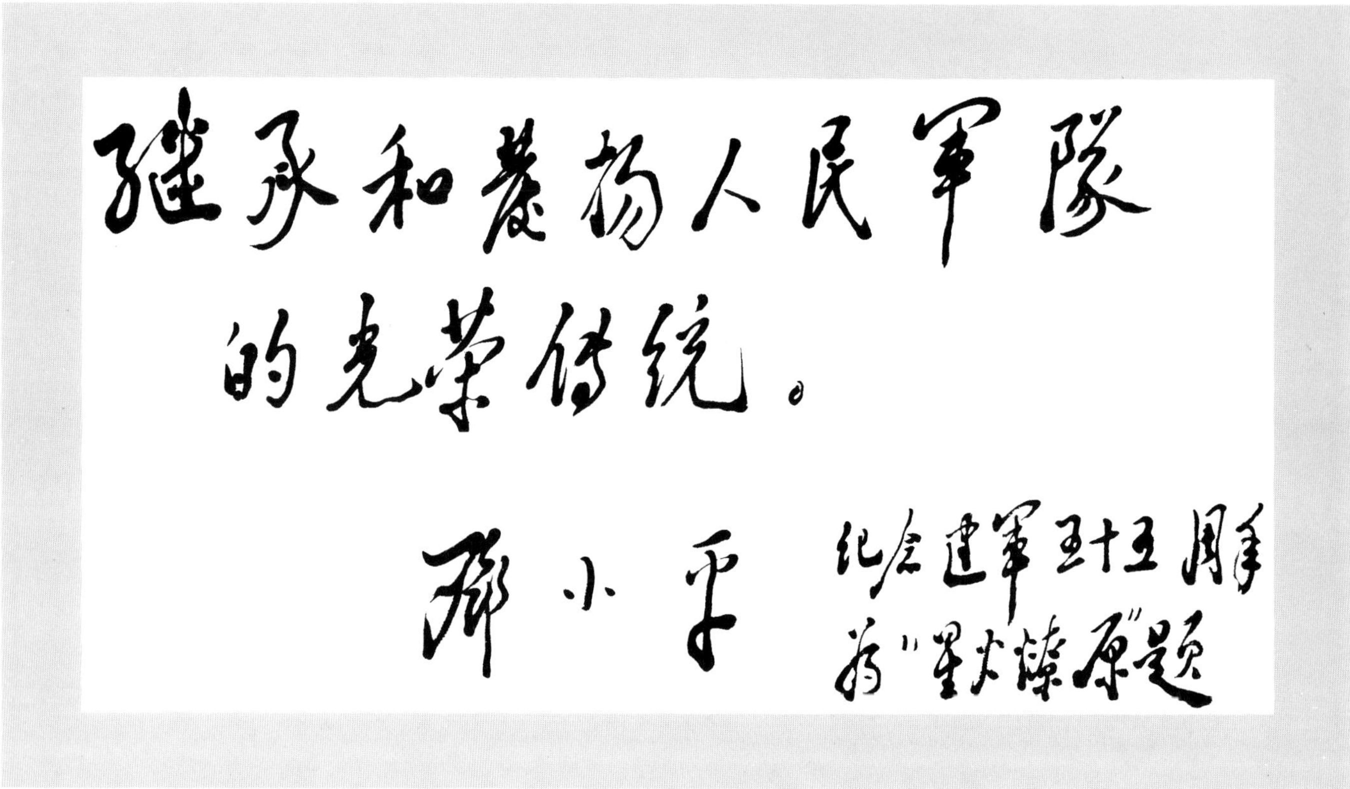

20

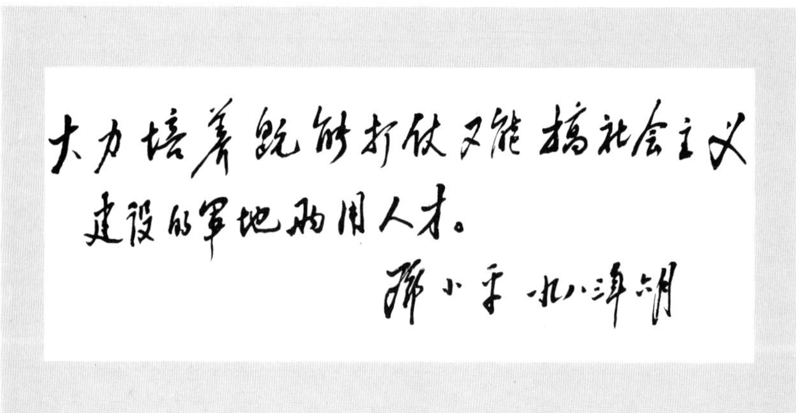

21

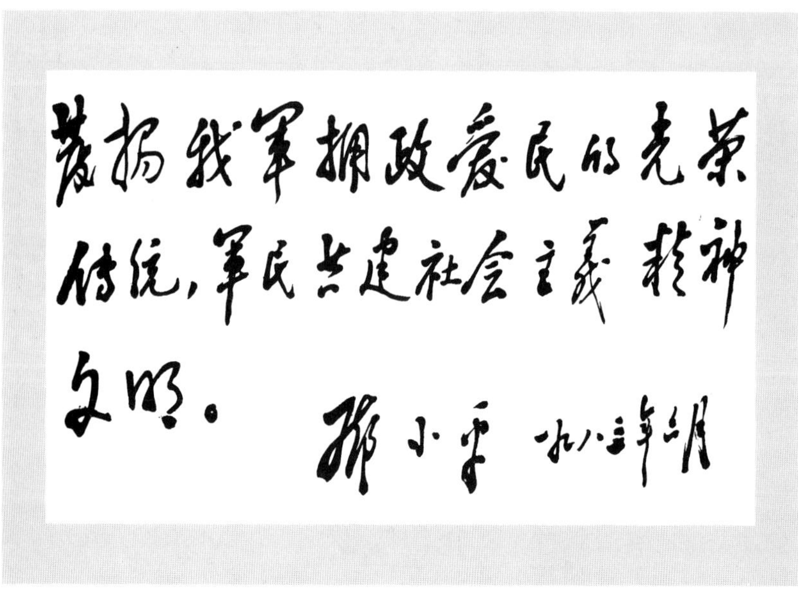

22

20. On the occasion of the 55th anniversary of the founding of the People's Liberation Army, Deng Xiaoping wrote an inscription for the book entitled "A Spark Causes a Prairie Fire." The photo shows his calligraphy: Inherit and bring into full play the glorious traditions of the people's army.

21-22. The calligraphy by Deng Xiaoping: (21) Strive to train dual-purpose persons who not only can fight in the battlefield, but also can participate in the socialist construction. (22) Bring into full play the glorious traditions of our army of supporting the government and loving the people, and building the socialist spiritual civilization through cooperation between the army and the people.

23. On October 1, 1984, the grand rally and military review were held to celebrate the 35th anniversary of the founding of the People's Republic of China. The photo shows Deng Xiaoping, standing on the car, begin his review.

23

24. Deng Xiaoping, reviewing the three armed forces.

24

A01-3375
A01-3430

25

26

25. Deng Xiaoping waved his hands in salute to the reviewed troops.

26. Deng Xiaoping (right) and Qin Jiwei, the commander in chief of the reviewed troops, were on the rostrum of Tian An Men.

27. The grand spectacle of the military review.

27

中华人民共和国万岁
世界人民大团结万岁

28

28. On November 11, 1984, Deng Xiaoping (second from left at front row), Yang Shangkun (third from left), Yu Qiuli (first from left), and Yang Dezhi (fourth from left) receiving the participants of the symposium held by the Central Military Commission.

29. On January 26, 1985, Deng Xiaoping (fourth from right at second row) was photographed with officers and men of the naval warship while inspecting the South Sea Fleet.

30. In June 1985, Deng Xiaoping received the deputies attending the enlarged meeting of the Central Military Commission. Second from right is Zhang Zhen.

29

30

31. At the enlarged meeting of the Central Military Commission, Deng Xiaoping announced that within three years, the People's Liberation Army would reduce its strength by one million.

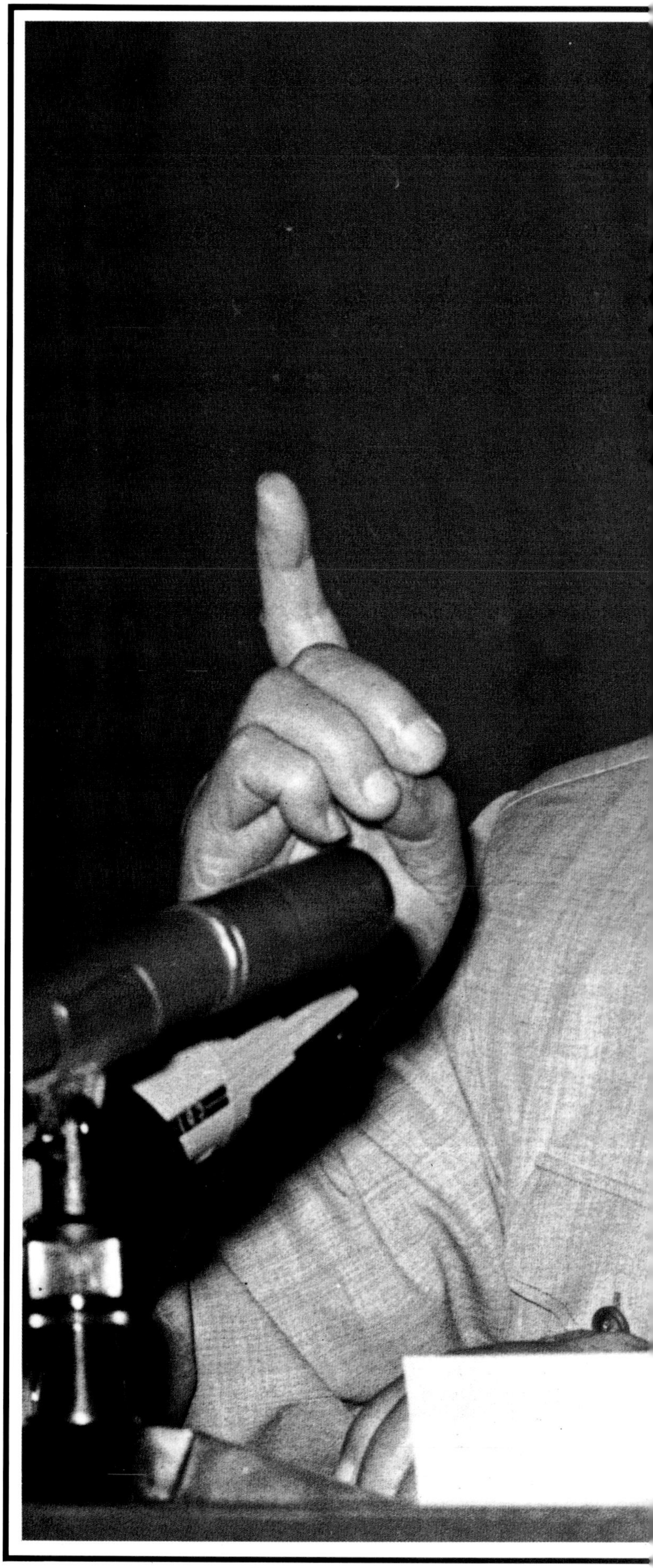

31

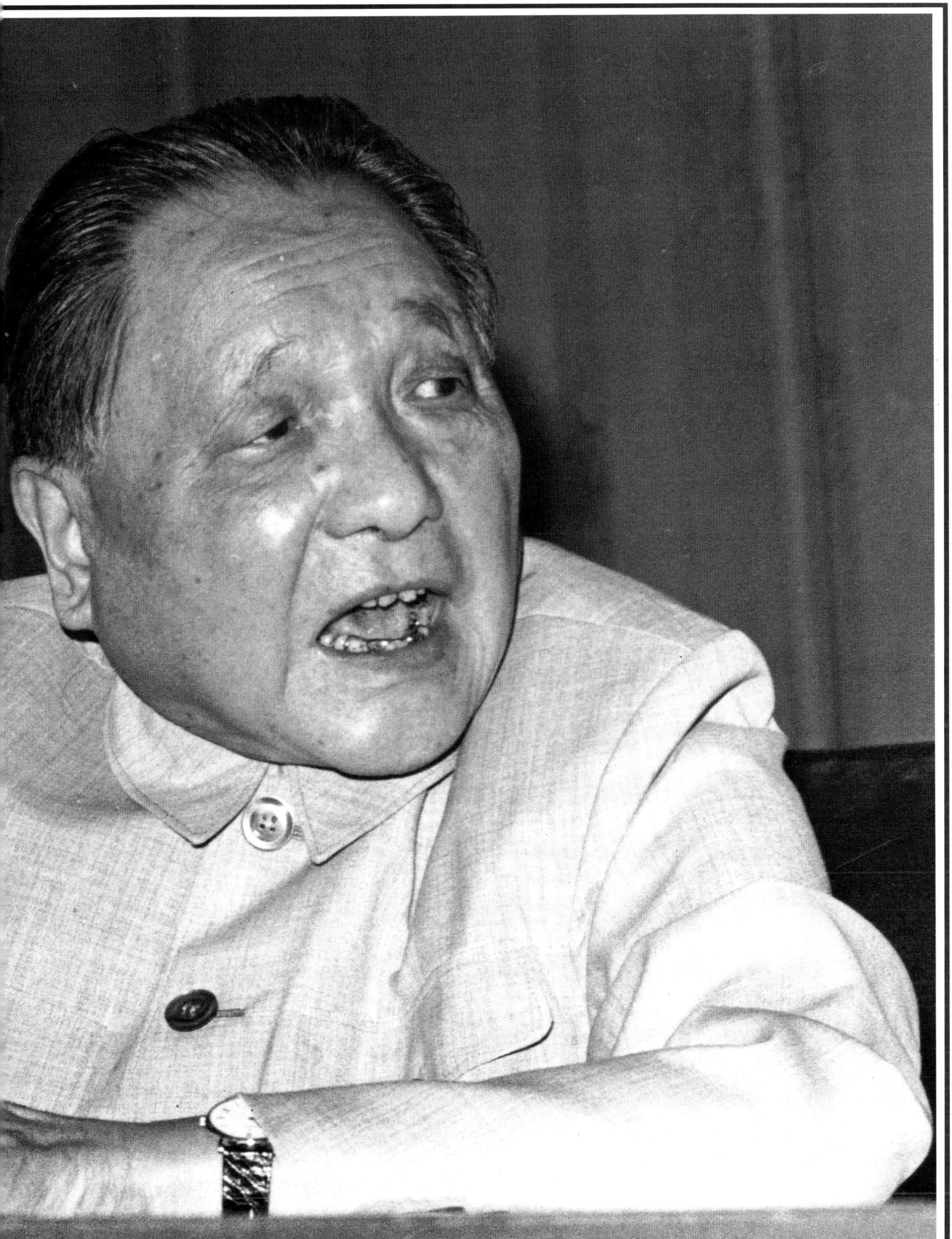

32

32. Deng Xiaoping looking at "Pictorial on the Liberation Army."

33. On October 7, 1986, Marshal Liu Bocheng passed away. During the years of war, Deng Xiaoping and Liu Bocheng fought shoulder to shoulder for 13 years. The photo shows Deng Xiaoping and his family members offering their condolences.

33

34

35

36

34. On December 25, 1986, Deng Xiaoping waved his greetings to the participants of the enlarged meeting of the Central Military Commission.

35. In December 1986, during the enlarged meeting of the Central Military Commission, Deng Xiaoping shook hands cordially with Nie Rongzhen.

36. Deng Xiaoping met with the participants of the enlarged meeting of the Central Military Commission. Zhang Aiping is on the right.

37. On July 31, 1987, Deng Xiaoping went to the Great Hall of the People to attend the activities to celebrate the 60th anniversary of the founding of the People's Liberation Army.

38. On July 31, 1987, Deng Xiaoping receiving the deputies of the heroes and exemplary fighters from the whole army.

39. The calligraphy by Deng Xiaoping on August 1, 1987: Strive to build our army into a powerful, modernized, and regularized revolutionary army.

40. On November 2, 1987, the First Plenary Session of the Party Thirteenth Central Committee was held in Beijing. Deng Xiaoping was once again elected unanimously to be Chairman of the Central Military Commission at the session.

37

38

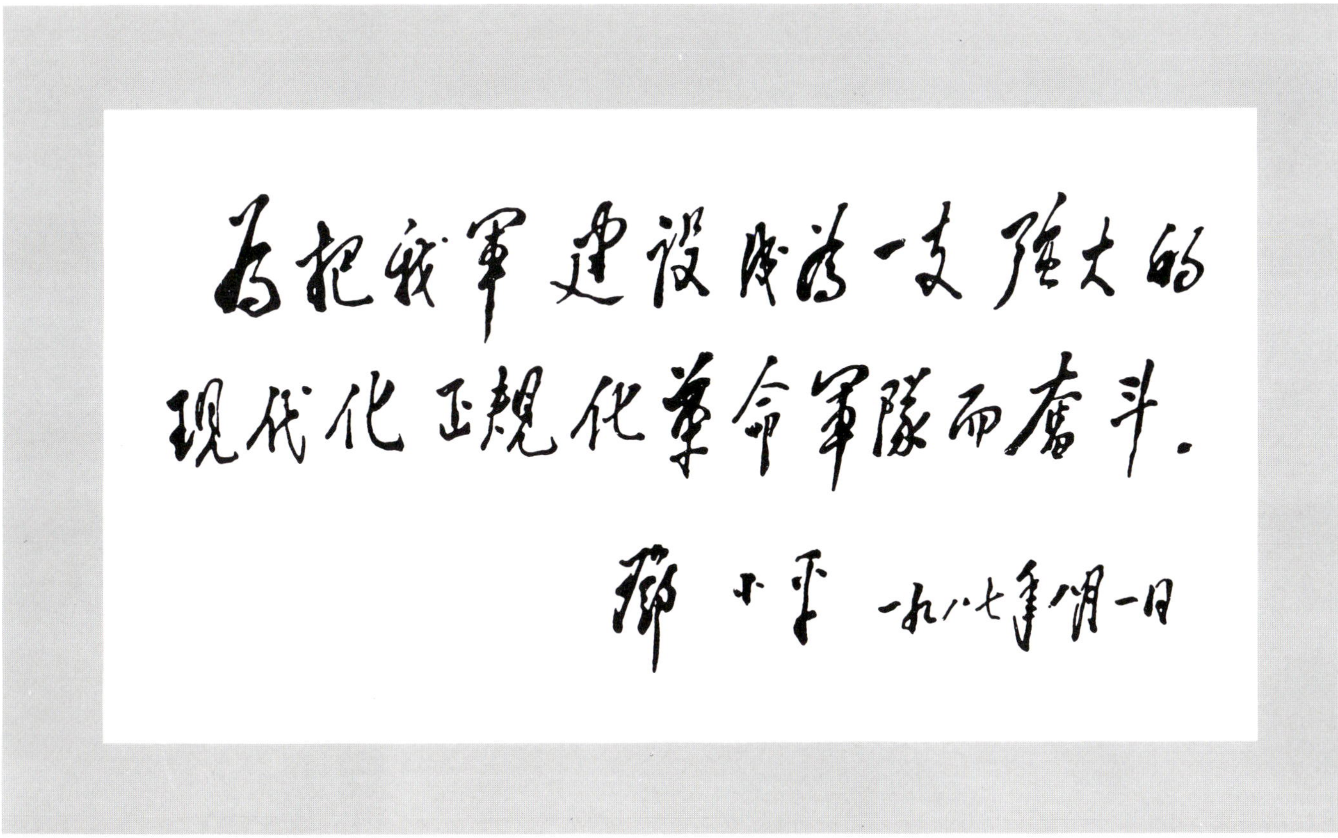

39

40

41

41. In July 1987, Deng Xiaoping had a cordial conversation with experts engaged in the scientific and technological work for the national defense.

42. In March 1988, Deng Xiaoping signed autographs for the deputies from the Armed Police attending the First Session of the Seventh National People's Congress.

43. In December 1988, Deng Xiaoping cordially received the deputies attending the enlarged meeting of the Central Military Commission.

42

43

44

44. In order to fulfill the requirements of realization of modernization in China, the Central Military Commission decided to restore the military ranking system. The photo shows that Deng Xiaoping, Li Xiannian (second from left), and others were cordially meeting with 17 high-ranking military officers who were the first batch to be granted the military ranking of general.

45

45. In June 1989, Deng Xiaoping, Li Xiannian (first from left), and others received the cadres at and above the level of army commander from the troops enforcing martial law in the Capital and made an important speech at the meeting.

Resigning from the Post of Chairman of the Central Military Commission of the Chinese Communist Party

1. In November 1989, accompanied by the new Chairman of the Central Military Commission Jiang Zeming (center) and the Vice-Chairman Liu Huaqing (right), Deng Xiaoping called on the participants of the enlarged meeting of the Central Military Commission.

In September 1989, Deng Xiaoping wrote a letter to the Political Bureau of the Party Central Committee and the National People's Congress, in which he expressed his sincere wishes that his request for resigning from the post of the Central Military Commission would be approved, and that he would like to take the lead in setting up the system of retirement.

The Fifth Plenary Session of the Party Thirteenth Central Committee, in its communiqué issued on November 9, 1989, decided to approve Deng Xiaoping's request for resigning from the post of Central Military Commission and decided that Jiang Zeming would be Chairman of the Central Military Commission. The session highly evaluated the outstanding contribution and remarkable feats Deng Xiaoping had accomplished for our Party, the nation, and the people's army.

The enlarged meeting of the Central Military Commission was held in Bejing from November 10 to 12, 1989. Jiang Zeming, Chairman of the Central Military Commission, pointed out at the meeting that all the achievements and progress made by our army in the past ten years were the results of the correct leadership of comrade Deng Xiaoping, and reflected on his wisdom and painstaking work. Now, comrade Xiaoping retired from the work post, but his thought and theory on the building of the army in the new era were our invaluable assets, and would play a long-term guiding role in the building of our army. We should study and implement them earnestly. On November 12, Deng Xiaoping met with all participants of the enlarged meeting of the Central Military Commission and demanded in his speech that the army should unswervingly maintain its nature, which meant that the army was the army of the Party, the people, and the socialist country. He also expressed that, though he left the army and retired, he would still pay close attention to the cause of the Party, the cause of the country, and the prospects of the army.

On November 20, 1989, Deng Xiaoping met with members and advisors of both the editorial committee and leading group for revision of *The War Annals of the Second Field Army of the Chinese People's Liberation Army*. He reminisced about the brilliant course of the Second Field Army during the revolutionary war years.

In March 1990, the Third Session of the Seventh National People's Congress adopted the decision to accept Deng Xiaoping's request for resigning from the post of Chairman of the Central Military Commission of the People's Republic of China and elected Jiang Zeming as the Chairman.

On November 5, 1991, the seminar on Deng Xiaoping's theory on the building of national defense and the building of the army in the new era jointly sponsored by the Military Science Academy and the Chinese Military Science Society was held in Beijing. Liu Huaqing, the Vice-Chairman of the Central Military Commission, pointed out in his opening remarks that comrade Deng Xiaoping, the core of the collective leadership of the second generation of our Party after the Third Plenary Session of the Party Eleventh Central Committee, was not only a chief architect for the cause of socialist modernization, but also a chief architect for the building of our national defense and the building of the army in the new era.

2. Deng Xiaoping shaking hands cordially with Jiang Zeming, the newly elected Chairman of the Central Military Commission.

2

3

3. Deng Xiaoping having a cordial conversation with Jiang Zeming after meeting with the participants of the enlarged meeting of the Central Military Commission.

4-5. Deng Xiaoping receiving the members of the leading group participating in compiling the War Annals of the Second Field Army.

4

5

6. On November 9, 1989, the Fifth Plenary Session of the Party Thirteenth Central Committee decided to approve Deng Xiaoping's request for resigning from the post of Chairman of the Central Military Commission. On November 12, Deng Xiaoping, together with Jiang Zeming, the new Chairman of the Central Military Commission, met with participants of the enlarged meeting of the Central Military Commission and made an important speech.

6

Route Map of 7th Army's Advances Towards the Central Revolutionary Base

October 1930-July 1931

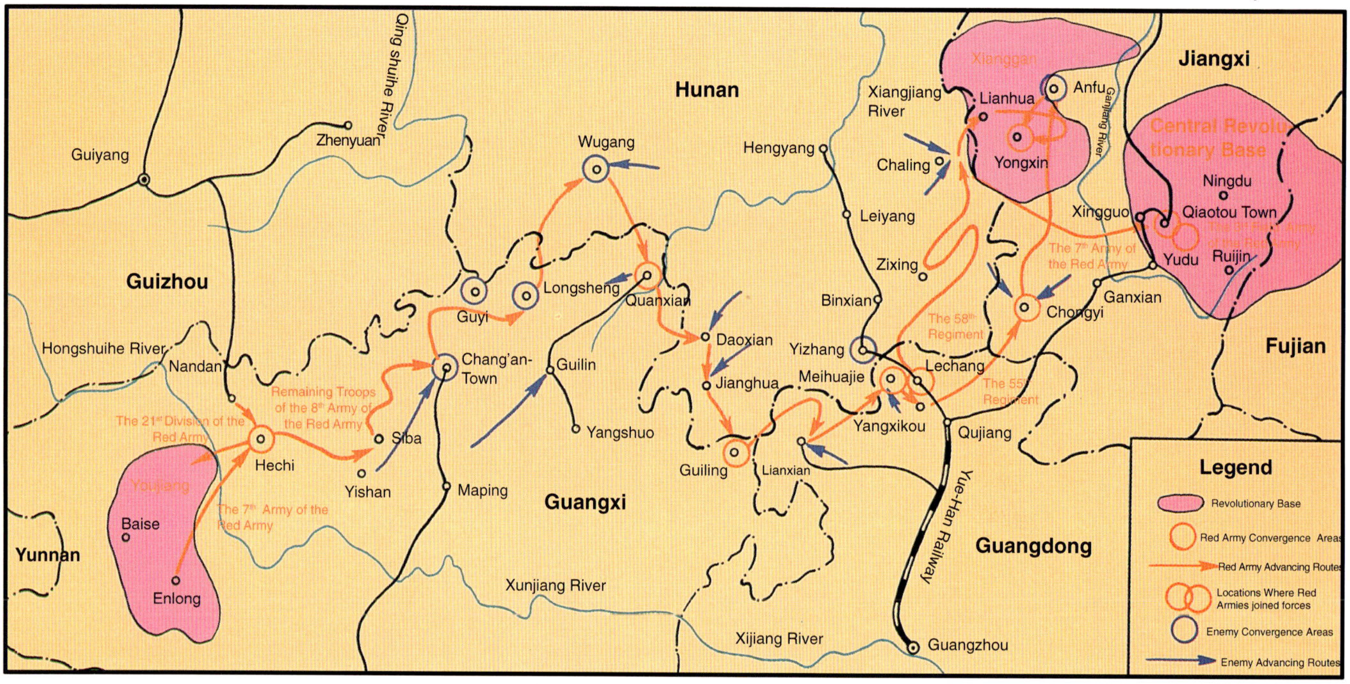

Mlilitary Geographic Map of the JinJiLuYu Librated Area

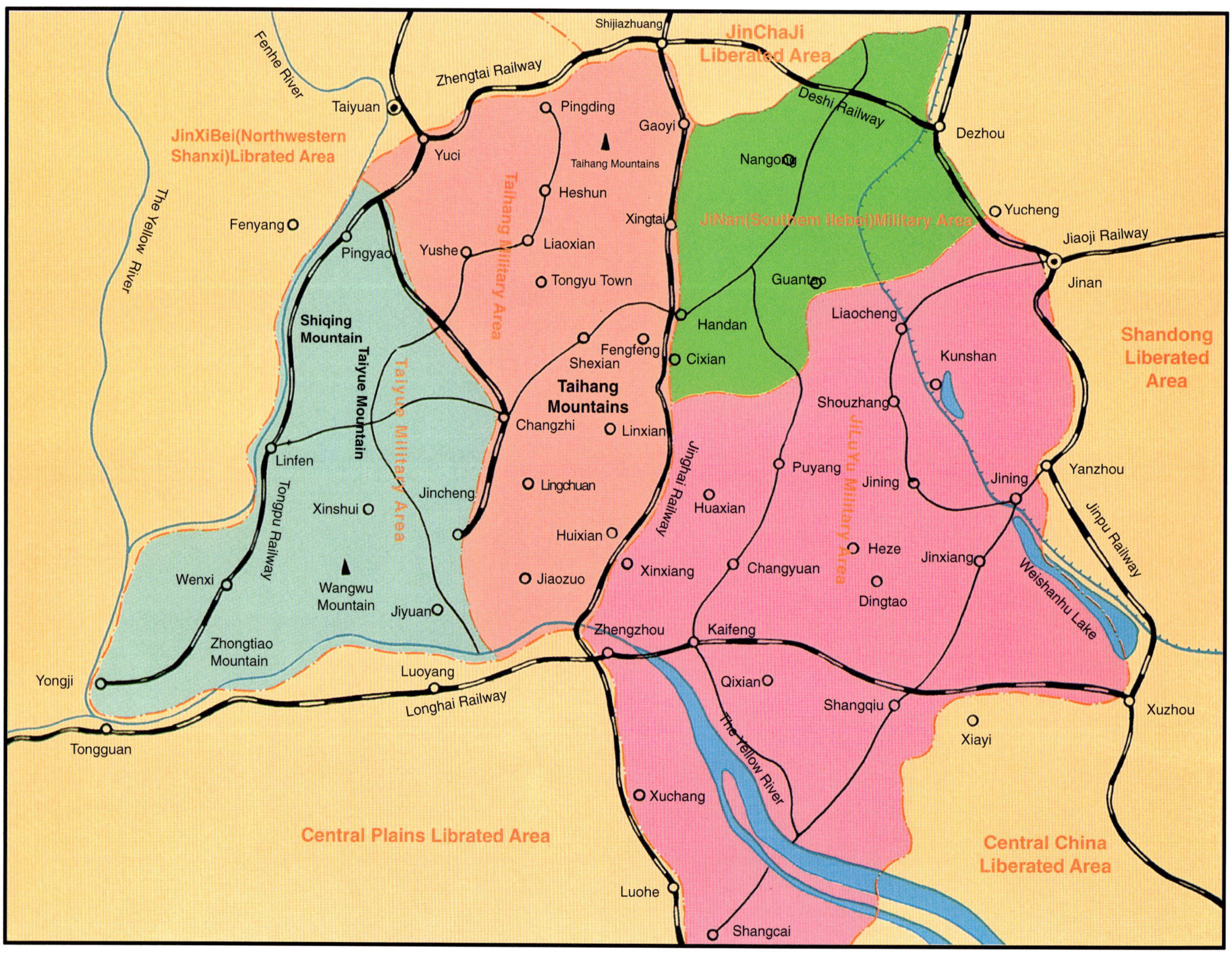

A Map About Deng Xiaoping's Military Activities in the Campaign of Advancing Towards Dabieshan Mountains, Huaihai Battle, Crossing-Yangtse River Battle and the Campaign of Advancing Towards the Southwest (June 1947 - October 1950)

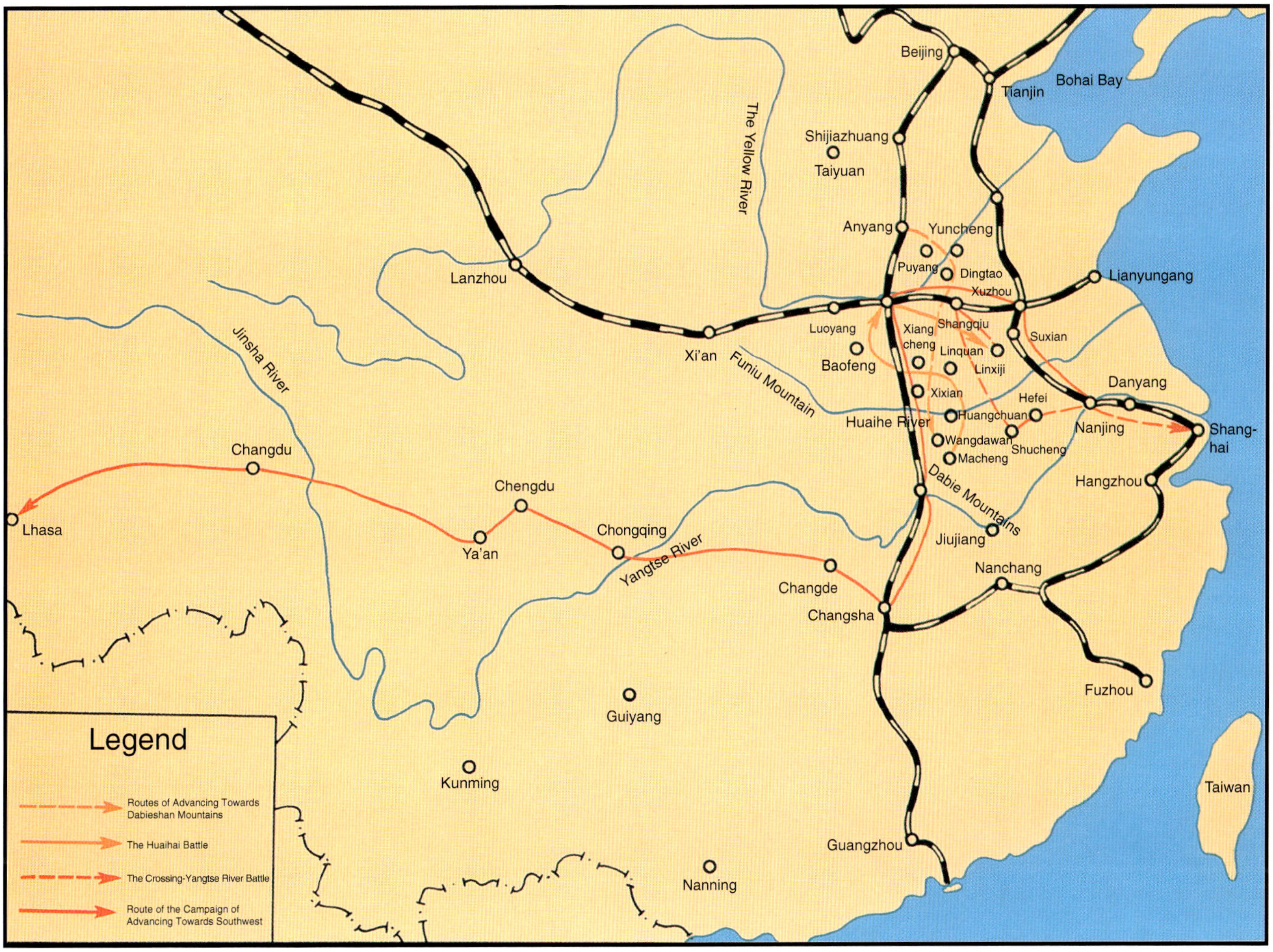

Editorial Board of Pictorial on Deng Xiaoping's Military Activities

Thanks to the Party Literature Research Center of the Central Committee of the Chinese Communist Party, the Editorial Department of the Pictorial on the Liberation Army and Chinese Photo Archives for their strong support and help to make it possible the publishing of this Pictorial.

Special thanks to:

Zhongjin Industrial Company, Ltd., Shenzhen

Chinese General Corporation of Supply, Marketing and Shipping of Non-ferrous Metal Products

Shenzhen Joint Futures Exchange of Non-ferrous Metal Goods

Chinese Great Wall Aluminum Company

Chinese Import and Export General Corporation of Non-ferrous Metal

Silver and Non-ferrous Metal Company

Zhuhai Xinguang Group Company, Ltd.

Hainan Jinhai Company, Ltd.

Guizhou Aluminum Plant

Xinyuan Non-ferrous Metal Development Company, Shantou Special Economic Zone